Table of Contents

Live Better, Live Well

We Can All Have an Impact on Childhood Health

We have an epidemic on our hands. One out of every three young people in the United States is already overweight or obese. As a result of a number of growing trends, including the convenience of fast food, the perceived high cost of healthier options, and a lack of access to resources that can help children and their families live better, this could be the first generation of kids who live sicker than their parents, largely because of a greater incidence of obesity-related health issues that also drive up the cost of health care. Childhood obesity is a tremendous drain on America's health care system. The health care industry spends $61 billion annually to treat obesity-related ailments, giving doctors, insurers, and employers a strong incentive to stop weight gain before it causes serious health problems.

There is no single cause and no single solution for childhood obesity. Because children have limited ability to control their own circumstances — where they go to school, which doctor they see, what type of snacks are available at home — any approach to eradicating childhood obesity must focus on systemic changes and address all the factors and environments that affect a child's life. To do that, we must work directly with industry leaders, educators, parents, doctors, and kids. If we want to stop this epidemic, we all have to step up and be a part of the solution.

A family focus on promoting healthier lives for our children

Health security has been one of the primary missions of my foundation since we started, and I have spent most of my life trying to help give children a better future. I get excited about any effort to promote healthier lives for our children. After my first heart surgery, I wanted to find some way to use that experience to help others. In 2005, my foundation partnered with the American Heart Association to create the Alliance for a Healthier Generation.

The goal of the Alliance is to reduce the prevalence of childhood obesity by 2015 and empower kids nationwide to make healthy lifestyle choices. We work to positively affect the places that can make a difference in a child's health: homes, schools, doctors' offices, and communities. The Alliance has made a tremendous impact since its inception seven years ago. We have:

- Worked with nearly 15,000 schools to transform their campuses into healthier places where healthier foods and enhanced physical activity opportunities are available before, during, and after school.
- Brokered voluntary agreements with the beverage, snack food, and dairy industries, resulting in a 90 percent decrease in the amount of beverage calories shipped to schools across the country and 30 million school children gaining access to healthier school meals.
- Increased health care access for more

than 2.6 million children through a landmark agreement with insurers, employers, and provider associations to reimburse physicians and registered dietitians for obesity prevention-related services and build the capacity of the health care workforce to support wellness and prevention.

• Worked with out-of-school time providers around the country to create healthy environments where youth can eat better and move more. These out-of-school time sites are implementing the Alliance healthy eating and physical activity standards to make the places where kids spend their time before school, after school, and during school breaks healthier.

Despite this progress, we are far from solving the childhood obesity epidemic. There is still so much work to be done. Families can play a big role in combatting and reversing childhood obesity and help kids become healthier adults. In this book, you will read about parents who have made changes in their own homes and in their communities to help their children lead healthier lives. You will read about youth who exemplify the key role that young people play in both engaging and educating their peers. Involving and honoring these incredible activists is an important step toward achieving a healthier America.

I have had the privilege of meeting many of the parents and young people featured in this book. I hope they will inspire you as much as they have me to take action in your own homes, schools, and communities. In the coming year, make your own plan for being well and take the steps necessary to improve the health of your family.

"Families can play a big role in combatting and reversing childhood obesity and help kids become healthier adults."

About President Bill Clinton

William Jefferson Clinton, the first Democratic president in six decades to be elected twice, led the United States to the longest economic expansion in U.S. history, including the creation of more than 22 million jobs.

After leaving the White House, President Clinton established the William J. Clinton Foundation with the mission to improve global health, strengthen economies, promote healthier childhoods, and protect the environment by fostering partnerships among governments, businesses, nongovernmental organizations, and private citizens to turn good intentions into measurable results. Today, the Foundation has staff and volunteers around the world working to improve lives through several initiatives, including the Clinton Health Access Initiative, which is helping more than 4 million people living with HIV/AIDS access lifesaving drugs. The Clinton Climate Initiative, the Clinton Development Initiative, and the Clinton Giustra Sustainable Growth Initiative are applying a business-oriented approach to fight climate change worldwide and to promote sustainable economic growth in Africa and Latin America. In the U.S., the Foundation is working to combat the alarming rise in childhood obesity through the Alliance for a Healthier Generation, and to increase small-business growth in underserved communities. The Clinton Global Initiative brings together global leaders to devise and implement innovative solutions to some of the world's most pressing issues. So far, more than 2,000 CGI commitments have improved the lives of more than 400 million people in 182 countries.

In addition to his Foundation work, President Clinton has joined with former President George

President Bill Clinton

H.W. Bush three times — after the 2004 tsunami in South Asia, Hurricane Katrina in 2005, and Hurricane Ike in 2008 — and with President George W. Bush in Haiti in the aftermath of the 2010 earthquake. The Clinton Foundation also supports economic growth, job creation, and education in Haiti.

President Clinton was born on August 19, 1946, in Hope, Arkansas. He and his wife Secretary of State Hillary Rodham Clinton have one daughter, Chelsea, and live in Chappaqua, New York.

A Year of Being Well

Messages from Families on Living Healthier Lives

Childhood obesity is one the most significant health threats to our children. The time to take action is now, and everyday heroes — those who are willing to stand up and make a difference — motivate me to help our nation's children learn healthy habits that will lead to longer and healthier lives. As I work with Michael, our children, and our family foundation to help families lead healthier lives, I'm inspired by all kinds of people around me every day who are doing what they can to live a healthier lifestyle.

There's the mom who can't find fresh produce in her local market, so she takes an hour bus ride each week to a farmers market to provide healthy options for her children. There's the P.E. teacher who helped launch a schoolwide initiative to keep students active. There are the local farmers who remain committed to producing fresh, healthy food in a world of fast-food chains and processed, microwavable meals. There are the kids who are becoming heroes among their peers by

> *"I'm inspired by all kinds of people around me every day who are doing what they can to live a healthier lifestyle."*

Susan's children Alexa, Zachary, Kira, and Juliette Dell

putting themselves on a healthy path one step at a time.

A few years ago, I had the opportunity to narrate a book about 15 outstanding moms who are working to instill healthy habits in their kids. I've been a healthy-living advocate all my life, but I quickly found out how much I had to learn from those amazing moms with simple yet impactful ideas about how to keep their kids healthy. The moms featured in the book don't have many of the resources that other moms do. What they do possess is the creativity and determination to guide their children toward the healthiest lives possible.

These women live in a combat zone of fast foods, sugar, limited access to safe places to be active, and the lure of electronic games and TV. Like many of us, they work. They juggle their children's schedules and all of the responsibilities of motherhood — in many cases single motherhood. But they care enough about their kids to make the extra effort it takes to ensure that they are getting the healthy foods and exercise they need.

These people are heroes because they are committed to providing a healthier lifestyle for their children and they believe in their own ability to change the lives of those around them.

Since the book was first printed, we've distributed 1.2 million copies to individuals, schools, health clinics, and community groups. And we've seen the ideas found in the book come to life in every state in the U.S.

When we asked people who read the book what else they needed to get started on the journey to better health, families told us that they were inspired by the stories in the book but needed help jump-starting changes in their own homes. They felt empowered by the book but finished reading it and often asked the question, "Now what?"

"I encourage you to find your inner hero."

This book about being well is intended to answer that question with a series of simple actions. It is intended to help you take a single step — one each month for a year — toward healthy living. There are specific examples of how moms, dads, and kids cut down on sugar-sweetened beverages, ate more fruits and vegetables, became more physically active, and started movements in their schools and communities. These families have also shown us that being healthy doesn't necessarily mean being thin.

This new book is also meant to give you some resources where you can find even more information on eating and living better.

To make it easier for families to start down the path of fueling for performance and training for life, I wanted to share more concrete examples of the ways families incorporated healthier foods and plenty of physical activity into their daily lives. Making big life changes can seem daunting, but it doesn't have to be.

It's important for families to understand that small, easy steps can significantly increase our children's prospects for longer, healthier lives. My personal philosophy is "Fuel for Performance, and Train for Life." If we think of food as fuel, the right kind of fuel — or nutritious food — gives our children's bodies energy and their brains the nutrition they need to perform at their best. When their bodies are fueled through healthful eating habits — drinking plenty of water, eating palm-sized portions of lean meats, fat-free or low-fat dairy foods, a variety of fruits and vegetables, and whole grains — their bodies will perform better. If we can teach our children to fuel for performance, and train for life, they will be able to think and feel at their best when taking a test, playing music, painting a picture, participating in a sporting event, or engaging in other activities.

Being healthy is also about being physically active to train for life. Training for life means get moving, every day. Ride a bike, dance, swim, participate in a school sport, or walk to a friend's house. Small steps, literally, and fitting in physical activity every day help our children's bodies avoid serious health issues like heart disease and diabetes. If our children engage in daily exercise, they will live longer, healthier lives.

As you read this book about inspiring families, I encourage you to find your inner hero. Volunteer in a school program. Exercise with your children. Look for ways to build a healthy community in which your children can thrive. And get started on your family's year of being well.

About Susan Dell

Susan is a co-founder and Chairman of the Board of the Michael & Susan Dell Foundation. The foundation is dedicated to improving the lives of children living in urban poverty around the world. With offices in Austin, Texas, New Delhi, India, and Cape Town, South Africa, the Dell family foundation funds programs that foster high-quality public education and childhood health and improve the economic stability of families living in poverty. In the U.S., the foundation also funds childhood obesity prevention programs and a college scholarship program that recognizes academic potential and determination in students that have a definite need for financial assistance.

The foundation has committed more than $825 million to global children's issues and community initiatives to date.

Outside of her daily professional responsibilities, Susan competes in marathons, triathlons, and cycling races. Her most recent accomplishments include: setting the record for women (all age categories) and men (all age categories) on the bike stress test at the Cooper Institute in Dallas, Texas, in April 2012; first woman finisher in the 2009 Kaloko Cycling Race to La La Land in Kona, Hawaii; first woman finisher while setting a new course record for women in the 2007 Kaloko Sprint Cycling Race in Kona, Hawaii; first woman finisher while setting a new course record for women in the 2006 Sea To Stars Mauna Kea Road Race in Kona, Hawaii; setting the record in the 2007 40 to 44 women's age group for the Cooper Clinic stress test in Dallas, Texas; finished first place overall

Susan Dell

for men and women while setting the course record for women in 2004, a record which she then broke in 2007 in the Kaloko La La Land Cycling Race, in Kona, Hawaii; and she successfully competed in the 2003 Ironman World Championships.

Susan was a member of the President's Council for Physical Fitness and Sports, is a trustee of the Children's Medical Center Foundation of Central Texas, and a board member of the Cooper Institute in Dallas. She and her husband, Michael, live in Austin, Texas, with their four children.

Featured Families

David is a stay-at-home dad in Austin, Texas. He lives with his wife, Anne, and their 13-year-old son, Jesse.

Ashlyn is 16 years old, has two sisters, and lives in New Orleans, Louisiana, with her parents.

Stevon is a dad from Nashville, Tennessee. He and his wife have two young daughters, Sanai and Mariset.

Donnie is a special education teacher who lives in Boston, Massachusetts, with his wife and sons, Austin and Mateo.

Guido is a 12-year-old who lives in Miami, Florida, with his parents and younger brother, Tomas.

Debra is a mother of two girls. She and her daughter, Giovanni, live together in New York, New York.

Sonora has two sons, Quavis Jr. and Troy, and one grandson. She lives with her husband in Atlanta, Georgia.

Lakeysha resides in San Diego, California. She and her husband have three kids, Elijah, Namaya, and Victor.

Jovita lives in Chicago, Illinois. She has four children, Cindy, Luis, Emmanuel, and Roberto.

Rochelle is a mother of seven who lives in Philadelphia, Pennsylvania. Her children are Armoni, Cavhanah, Adoniyah, Keziah, Keturah, Bashira, and Iman.

Featured Families

Rosa lives in Chicago, Illinois, with her husband and four children, Evon, Evelyn, Romero, and Juan.

Jamilia is a mother of five, Zephariah, Zaniya, Zaire, Zakari, and Zianna. She lives in Oakland, California.

Emilia, her husband, and her children, Sergio, Jessica, Juan, and Anthony, live in Austin, Texas.

Wendy is a mom from Houston, Texas. She lives there with her family, including her three daughters, Liz, Jessi, and Katie.

Cindy lives near Detroit, Michigan, with her husband and three kids, Austin, Samantha, and Zack.

Xinia is a mother who lives in San Diego, California, with her husband and teenage children, Xinia and Felix.

Ashley resides in Houston, Texas. She lives there with her husband and sons, Avery and Julian.

Angie lives in Harrisburg, Pennsylvania, with her husband and four children, Tim, Prem, Jyoti, and Mahesh.

Gaye is a mom from Denver, Colorado, who lives with her husband and daughters, Taylor, Rachel, and Mya.

Andrea lives in Tucson, Arizona. She is a mother of four kids, Roman, Mickey, Desiree, and Alex.

MONTH

1

Get
Started

Everyone has to start somewhere, but it always seems like getting started is the hardest part of doing anything. I've found that people make changes to their habits for a lot of different reasons. Sometimes they are forced to change because of a health scare. Sometimes a family member's situation makes people see changes necessary for themselves. Sometimes, people living in similar neighborhoods or environments simply encourage them to adopt healthier habits.

Once we decide to change our habits, there are practical questions to address: When should we start something new? When should we introduce a new vegetable at dinner? When should we kick off a family evening walk? It all depends on what works for your family. There is no right or wrong answer. But it is important that you think about your family's lifestyle and incorporate changes — at the right time and pace — in ways that will increase your chances for success.

You'll see that the families in this book all started making changes at different times for different reasons. They live in different areas, their family dynamics are different, and they faced different challenges when trying to lead healthier lives in their communities. The most successful families are often the families that adopt new habits together — mom and dad play with the kids instead of sending them outside to play alone or stop drinking soda when they expect their children to do the same. But they all started from the same place you are at now: the beginning. — *Susan Dell*

Did **you** know?

80 percent of obese children ages 10 to 13 become obese as adults.
American Academy of Child & Adolescent Psychiatry

Being overweight or obese raises the risk of colon, breast, endometrial, and gallbladder cancers.
National Heart Lung and Blood Institute

Jamilia
and her family

Jamilia is from a large, loving family, but some of her dearest family members became examples of what she didn't want to be. Even though she's a single, employed mother who also takes courses to further her education, she started to get her family on the right track by educating herself so she could improve her own health first. She began incorporating healthy foods and plenty of exercise into the lives of her five young children. Jamilia is now helping other families by educating others in her Oakland community. She even helped organize a group of parents to work together to make sure they had access to affordable produce. It all happened because she took the first step of deciding that changes needed to happen in her life. — *Susan Dell*

"I realized I had to be ambitious enough to see my children grow old. I look forward to being here for my kids. They make me have ambition to do other things. If I can start them off right, they'll end up right.

I come from a large family, and we really love to eat. When I was little, we'd have family meals with fried chicken, fried pork chops, fried steak ... It seemed like everything we ate was fried. But then my mom got Type 2 diabetes, and both of my grandmothers had diabetes. When my Grandma Olivia died of complications from diabetes, I looked at myself and realized I had to make changes for myself and my kids. I didn't want to die from the same disease. I didn't want my kids to have to worry about losing me too early.

We started making slow, small changes. I substituted healthier ingredients in recipes I knew my kids already liked. I started using ground turkey in place of ground beef. I started adding peas and carrots to pasta or tuna casserole I knew they'd eat. The more I involved them in the planning and cooking, the more they'd try different things. They came around.

I woke up to the fact that I could either wait to be the problem, or I could start now and prevent a problem from happening."

Sonora
and her family

Sonora took a very different approach to hitting "reset" on her family's habits. Sonora, her husband, and two sons were forced to make immediate and drastic adjustments to their diets and exercise routines when one son was diagnosed with a heart condition as a teenager. It took a lot of strength, a lot of patience, and a lot of good food to feed her growing boys' minds, bodies, and souls.
– Susan Dell

"It all started with a trash bag. It took a health crisis to get us to change the habits in our home, but the first step toward making all of the changes we needed to make was to pick up a trash bag. I threw away all of the bad foods. I couldn't allow my son to eat fried or unhealthy foods anymore, so I decided we were going to change our habits as a family.

I had to look at every day as a learning experience. To make sure I filled the kitchen with the right foods, I went on the Internet and looked up which foods I should get. I looked at brochures from the hospital. I talked to my friends. I went to the YMCA and got information. I did all I could to get as much knowledge as I could. Yes, it was a lot of work. But it was worth it. Yes, I spent a little more money on fresh foods. But it was all for my son, and he's worth more to me than anything.

It didn't take me long to realize that my son was the one with the heart problem, but I was the one who was really responsible for helping him make the biggest, most important changes in his life. I'm the mother. I control the car keys, the money, and the shopping list. If I don't buy it, my kids won't eat it. I had to learn to stand in the store and read labels. I had to start preparing better for each day so I always had healthy snacks in the car instead of always having to drive through a fast-food restaurant. It was all my responsibility. And I learned to love it."

Gaye
and her family

Gaye has been nimble enough to change her own habits to maintain a healthy weight. She's also managed to incorporate healthy foods and plenty of exercise into the routines of three daughters, who span a 14-year age difference, and has kept trying new things with a husband who has been slow to adjust to a healthier way of living. — *Susan Dell*

"After reaching a weight of 200 pounds, I started a new life chapter by losing weight and focusing my attention on the permanence of maintaining this change. As an African-American mom of three daughters, I have kept the weight off because I believe they deserve to see what a healthy lifestyle really looks like up close and to understand that it can exist for people who look like them. This can be an extremely difficult task with a culture that celebrates 'super-size' portions.

As a mom with a career, husband, and three daughters, neither nutrition or physical activity are a given. I must work to define, create, and advocate for a healthy lifestyle to ensure my children get the message.

For my youngest daughter, a healthy beginning was a chance to set a different course for her life starting as young as elementary school. I've established a 'new normal' that involves exercise as a fixed part of the day. I'm teaching her that 'strong' is a powerful self-defining adjective and that an avoidance of candy, soda, and high-fat foods is just the way we should eat.

For each of my teenagers, health has meant two different things. What two teenagers are alike? For my middle daughter, our healthy lifestyle has sparked a new appreciation for the benefits of exercise and physical activity. For my oldest (one who does not necessarily like to exercise), it has meant growing in the knowledge of what constitutes physical activity. She tried things like joining a dance class and getting up in the morning to do yoga.

Dad has started, too! He would be described as a slow adopter, but he's coming along. The key for him has been small changes."

4

EASY STEPS TO
be well
this month

1 **Pick a start date that works** for you and your family. It might be a Monday, the beginning of a month, or the first day your family can meet and be active together on a weekly basis. You can also **start today**!

2 Set aside an **hour each week to research** ways to be healthier, such as new recipes, new activities to do with your family, free resources available in your community, or ways to **track your progress**. Research doesn't have to be hard. **Ask** family members and friends who are already taking healthy steps for their advice, search the Internet, or ask the nutrition director at your child's school for ideas. **Planning** will make your transition smoother.

3 Don't get frustrated. **Big changes take time**. Take **small steps** each day and do your best. If you have a bad day, start again tomorrow!

4 Tell someone that you are making **healthy changes** and share some of the ways you plan to lead a **healthier life**. You'll be more motivated to **stick to your goals**, and you might just find a partner to encourage you during your journey.

Important tips:
• Small steps can have a big impact.
• Choose one or two steps to begin each month.

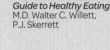

Resources

PUBLICATION

Eat, Drink, and Be Healthy: The Harvard Medical School Guide to Healthy Eating
M.D. Walter C. Willett, P.J. Skerrett

MOBILE APP

Family Meals by More Time Moms

ORGANIZATION

American Academy of Pediatrics
www.healthychildren.org

COMMUNITY

Your community health clinic

Get Smarter

Many resources exist to help families learn about healthy foods and the importance of physical activity. But finding the information requires you to take the initiative to start looking for the answers to the questions you have.

Start by writing down your questions. For instance, what are the first habits I should try to instill in my children to improve their health? How do I get started with an exercise program? Where can I get affordable fruits and vegetables in my community? How do I keep my family motivated to maintain healthy habits for a lifetime?

There are resources in every community in America — many of them are free — that can help you in your quest for a healthy lifestyle.

Ask your doctor or local health clinic for information on healthy habits and collect the free materials they have available. Go to your local library and access the Internet to find farmers markets in your community. Participate in a local community garden or walking club.

Half of the children in our country don't have a park or community center in their neighborhood. Even so, there are books in your local library and online resources that can give you ideas on how to get exercise indoors. Resources are available everywhere. If you live in a climate that limits the amount of time your kids can spend playing outside, visit your local YMCA. Learn about activities you can do with your children in your own home. Talk to other parents who face the same challenges you do. Get ideas from healthy friends and neighbors.

Learn from other parents, friends, and your own children. You'll be surprised what you can teach each other. – *Susan Dell*

Did **you** know

The proportion of obese children 5 to 17 years old was five times higher in 2008 to 2009 than in 1973 to 1974.
American Heart Association

More than one-third of U.S. adults (35.7 percent) are obese.
Centers for Disease Control and Prevention

Jovita
and her family

As a mother of four, Jovita is leading the charge when it comes to teaching others what she learned herself. After using free community health classes to combat her own health risks and change her children's unhealthy habits, she began teaching nutrition and healthy cooking in her community. It was clear to her that someone needed to stand up and promote healthy foods and regular physical activity among her friends and neighbors. — *Susan Dell*

"I live in a Latino neighborhood in Chicago called Little Village. A few years ago, I felt like every time I looked around, I saw more and more obese kids. I saw my friends' children developing diabetes at a young age, and I didn't understand how this could be happening.

When I started doing my research, I saw that other neighborhoods had healthy school lunches that included more fruits and vegetables. I knew that we didn't have healthy lunch options at our own schools, and that I had to get involved and educate the schools and parents on the foods our kids needed to be eating.

I started by standing outside schools and asking parents to join me. I had to talk about the healthy changes I'd made and get the parents to understand how their own choices were affecting their kids. I then worked with the Little Village Environmental Justice Organization and Healthy Schools Campaign's Padres Unidos Para Escuelas Saludables (Parents United for Healthy Schools) to organize groups of people to teach each other about eating healthy and becoming more active. We started walking groups, gardening clubs, and exercise classes. We organized groups of people who could learn about healthy habits on their own, and then come to the group and share what they learned.

The people in our neighborhood also worked together to develop a cookbook with healthy versions of traditional foods. The cookbook helped us learn how to make traditional Latin dishes in a healthier way.

The changes in our community have been fantastic. I learned how to take better care of myself by learning from others and sharing what they taught me with an even bigger group of people."

Ashlyn

and her family

Ashlyn is one of the most resourceful 16-year-olds I've encountered. A few years ago, she learned that she was overweight and was motivated enough to do something about it. Now it seems that she does whatever she can to help others lead a healthier lifestyle by sharing the things she's learned with anyone who will listen. — *Susan Dell*

"The first thing that made me want to live a healthier lifestyle happened when I was younger. I was overweight and out of shape. We went to the doctor, and he told me to stop drinking sugary soft drinks and start eating better. I was surprised how much those little changes really helped. I then got involved with Lighten Up Louisiana. It was a website that helped me track my water intake and the nutrition values of the foods I was eating. It really opened my eyes to the difference between good foods and junk foods.

I went to my high school and asked them to allow other students to start using the Lighten Up Louisiana program. In P.E., students started tracking the activity they did and what they ate each day. The more involved I got in trying to get students to use the program, the more healthy habits I learned and the more I benefited.

I've also tried to find other groups and programs that could help me get healthier. I started exercising more, and the more I exercised the easier it was. Now I play soccer, run track, and do cheerleading. If I stopped watching what I ate and got too heavy, I know I wouldn't be able to perform well. My coaches give us workouts to do while we're at home and teach us to be active even when we're not practicing with the team.

I want people to know what I've learned: By getting healthy and staying healthy, you can feel better and do better at a lot of things. Even though it is a challenge to live a healthier lifestyle, it pays off in the long run."

Gaye
and her family

Gaye is helping her three daughters learn about healthy food choices and the importance of physical activity. She learned from her own mistakes and educated herself on healthy ways to feed her family and keep them active. From climbing the Red Rock Mountains to enforcing healthy eating habits in her own home with a "no soda and candy allowed" rule, the mission is nutrition and health, and it's a dish served nightly. — *Susan Dell*

"My concern for my family's health habits came after I was successful in changing my own unhealthy habits, which helped me to lose weight and reduce my risk for chronic disease. I realized how much time and money I had spent on diets, and I wanted to work to help my daughters to not repeat my mistakes.

Growing up, my family did include vegetables with meals, but there was not an emphasis on the nutritional balance or avoiding saturated fats, sugar, etc. We are much more conscious of reading nutrition labels now and understanding how to put foods together to create healthy meals.

My oldest daughters were in elementary school when I first started trying new approaches like limiting fast foods and prepackaged items for lunches and snacks. Of course, over the years, I've gotten smarter, and with my youngest, I have just avoided even going down certain unhealthy roads with her. For ex-

ample, she has never had soda, and I am really trying to hold the line on that one. By the time she can make choices away from home, I'm hoping that the desire just won't be there.

I make an effort to cook my meals and prepare healthy snacks at home. I use fruit as a dessert or treat. I puree vegetables and include them in sauces, casseroles, and breads. I choose to limit the number of times that we eat out. I teach my family how to make good decisions about portion size and foods.

I also learned to get the entire family involved in meal preparation, especially dinner, which is when I need help the most. We all enjoy finding new recipes in magazines and cookbooks and then preparing them.

Overall, I think our family has adjusted to the healthy changes pretty well. My kids support my personal ideals to eat healthy, and they get the big picture of how our daily choices influence our health."

4

EASY STEPS TO
be well
this month

1 Ask your doctor for **free pamphlets** and information on **healthy habits**.

2 Visit your local library or free computer lab and go online to **find food trackers** that you can use to track your foods, water intake, and physical activity.

3 Find a friend or family member who has instilled healthy habits in their home and get ideas from them. You can **learn** so much **from their experiences**.

4 Try to **reward children** with stickers, a puzzle, or even a book instead of food items.

Important tips:
• Small steps can have a big impact.
• Choose one or two steps to begin each month.

Resources

PUBLICATION

The Monster Health Book: A Guide to Eating Healthy, Being Active, and Feeling Great for Monsters and Kids! Edward Miller

MOBILE APP

SmartCalories

ORGANIZATION

American Heart Association
www.heart.org

COMMUNITY

Your local public library

Lead
by Example

S tudies have shown that much of the learning that occurs during development is gained through observation and imitation. While kids look to friends, celebrities, and athletes to be role models, as parents, we still have an enormous amount of influence on our children's lives. Our kids are more likely to imitate our good behavior if we spend time with them and are intentional about what we want to model.

Throughout my involvement in the Be Well project, I'm continually reminded that we all seem to learn best through examples of people like us. We look at those around us, identify common goals, relate to common challenges, and use the successes of others to help shape our own stories.

The parents featured in this book are from all across the United States. Their children range in ages from 2 to 26. They each faced different obstacles when trying to improve their children's overall health, and they shared their stories simply because they wanted to help other families.

The parents in this book each started instilling healthy habits by adopting good habits themselves. They could then be credible resources and role models for their own children — and for other parents who want their children to be well.

The kids in this book are trendsetters in their own right. They took it upon themselves to get smarter about healthy living, to start moving, to play more, and model the healthy habits. — *Susan Dell*

Did **you** know?

Research shows that when parents increase their physical activity, children increase theirs as well.
Journal of Physical Activity and Health (July 2012)

Parental fruit and vegetable intake may be the strongest predictor of fruit and vegetable consumption among young children.
National Institutes of Health

Ashley
and her family

Ashley never thought she'd be a runner, but she's always wanted to be a good mother. Now, she's both.

Ashley learned about the benefits of running from her own father, but she didn't start running herself until her children were in elementary school. Each day she ran a little bit farther, until she achieved her first major milestone of running a 10K. Now her two sons are following in her footsteps and run with her in their Houston-area neighborhood every day. *– Susan Dell*

"There is nothing I want more in this world than for my boys to be the best they can be and as healthy as they can be. It's my job to give them the life tools they'll need now, so they're more likely to make good decisions later.

One of the things I've tried to teach them is something my dad taught me — the importance of exercise. I've put an emphasis on what exercise is and also what it isn't. It doesn't have to be painful. It is something that can be fun, and it is something we can do together every day.

My boys have a lot of energy. We needed an activity that we could all enjoy outside together. So every night, we go running as a family. My husband and I both work, but we make the time to have dinner with the boys, do homework, and run for at least an hour before we call it a night. We also try to eat well, and we'll sometimes have a treat. But you won't see us eating a piece of pizza without going out and exercising afterward.

You won't see me send my boys out to run by themselves. They look to me for guidance, so I'm going to lead them as well as I can as they are running down our street or down the road of life."

Cindy

and her family

Cindy involved her family from the moment she was diagnosed with Type 2 diabetes. She knew that she had to involve them in the process of changing their lifestyle and get their ideas on ways they thought their family could be healthier. *– Susan Dell*

"When I was diagnosed with Type 2 diabetes, I knew I'd need the support of my entire family. But they were all looking to me to be their example. They needed mom to be the one — to be the real person they knew who could get healthier. So I had to be the first person in our family to make changes and the last person who would allow anyone to get by with eating junk or following the same unhealthy path I had been on.

It was easier for me to make the changes that needed to be made because I knew my entire family was watching me: my mom, my husband, my three kids, other people in our family. They watched me gain weight, and they gained it right along with me. I figured if they watched me lose it and get healthy, they'd lose weight and get healthy with me, too."

Lakeysha
and her family

Lakeysha didn't consider herself to be a healthy mom. She just felt that it was her responsibility to make sure that her kids were eating the right things and doing plenty of physical activity. She not only tries to instill healthy habits, she makes sure that they understand what it means to live a healthy life.
— *Susan Dell*

"For me I really believe that leaving a healthy legacy for my family is important. When I'm long gone, I want them to have in their minds what they should do to live a healthy life and then teach their families to live a healthy life. I make sure they know the benefits of eating fruits and vegetables and how important it is to not only do physical activity but to enjoy it. I let them pick out things that they enjoy doing so they'll stay active.

Awhile ago, I was trying to teach my kids how to run and how to enjoy it. At first they didn't like it. They wanted to do other things.

So it became a give-and-take. I tried the things they enjoyed — like skateboarding and swimming — and they kept trying running. Now they like running, and we do 5K races together.

I've tried to model good habits and behaviors for them, and they've responded to that. I love that we teach each other and play together to stay active. We are lucky enough to live in a place where we have a beach to come to and play. But even if we lived in a different climate, I'd try to keep them active by staying active with them. I'm just happy that we're healthy together."

4
EASY STEPS TO
be well
this month

1   Don't **expect** your family to do anything you don't do yourself.

2   **Be honest** with your family. For example, if you cheat on your plan, admit the mistake, talk about why you think you did it, **discuss ways** to avoid similar events in the future, and start where you left off. Everyone should **feel comfortable** sharing successes and challenges throughout the year of healthy living.

3   If possible, find nonsedentary **activities that you like doing together** as a family. Simply ask your kids what they would like to play. All of a sudden, exercise that might have been viewed as work will be seen as **something fun**.

4   You don't all have to like all of the same types of exercise, but carve out the **same time each day** to be active together.

Important tips:
• Small steps can have a big impact.
• Choose one or two steps to begin each month.

Resources

PUBLICATION

My Food Plan
Carole Lewis

MOBILE APP

The Walking Deck

ORGANIZATION

Centers for Disease Control and Prevention
www.cdc.gov

COMMUNITY

Your community center

Drop
Liquid Calories

With all of the advertisements for soda, sports drinks, fruit drinks, energy drinks, and other beverages that exist today, it's not surprising to learn that Americans at every age drink more sugary beverages than ever before. The calories in sugar-sweetened beverages are called "empty calories" because they have no nutritional benefit.

Eliminating empty calories from sugar-sweetened beverages can make an enormous impact on the quality of your diet. Sugar-sweetened beverages include any drinks with ingredients on the label that mean "sugar": agave nectar, cane sugar, corn sweetener, corn syrup, evaporated can juice, fruit juice concentrates, high-fructose corn syrup, fructose, honey, maple syrup, molasses, and sucrose. This includes soda, sports drinks, sweetened tea and coffee, energy drinks, fruit drinks, and other sweetened drinks.

Since the majority of calories from sugar-sweetened beverages are consumed at home, it's our job as parents to keep healthy beverage options available and ready for our families.

Along with dropping liquid calories, we must teach our children the importance of water. Water should be the primary beverage for children. Try serving nonfat or low-fat milk or water with meals to introduce the healthiest beverages in your home. – *Susan Dell*

Did **you** know?

Americans get more calories from sugary drinks than any other beverage choice.
United States Department of Agriculture

Sugar-sweetened beverages are the largest source of added sugars in the diets of U.S. youth.
Centers for Disease Control and Prevention

Sonora
and her family

Because of family health issues, Sonora had to change everything about her family's diet — including eliminating the majority of liquid calories she, her husband, and her sons were consuming. She encouraged her sons to drink healthy beverages by simply making them available in her home.

She also had a few tricks up her sleeve when the boys protested giving up whole milk because they liked the taste of it. — *Susan Dell*

"When the boys were young, I didn't have anyone teaching me how unhealthy some drinks can be. I thought that if they were drinking anything with the words 'milk' or 'juice' in it, then it must be healthy. Was I wrong!

When I started studying the types of foods my sons should be eating, I learned that what they drank was as important as the food they ate. They hated low-fat milk, and they drank soda all of the time. They were taking in so much sodium and added sugar, just from their drinks. So I had to trick them a little.

I read the labels on fruit juices to make sure they were 100-percent juice without added sugars. Instead of telling them right off the bat that I was going to start giving them low-fat milk, I gradually worked it in. I took a gallon of whole milk, poured that out, and replaced it with low-fat milk. They didn't even know the difference. A few weeks later, I told them they'd been drinking low-fat milk for weeks. That's what I had to do!

They tried to sneak soda at first. They'd go out or go to a friend's house, but then they got used to the healthier drinks. But the main thing I tried to do was get the boys to drink more water. I told them that water was the one drink they could have as much as they wanted.

My husband and I feel like we should all work together. So when my sons needed to change, we changed, too. We drank more water and skim milk. We stopped drinking the things we wouldn't let them drink."

Rosa
and her family

Rosa, a mom from Chicago, loves her children. They bring her a lot of joy. But a bout with severe depression left her overweight and in need of some drastic changes. So Rosa changed the things she ate and drank to get her weight under control and improve her family's overall health.

Rosa's children protested the new foods and beverages at first — they didn't want to stop drinking soda and energy drinks. But once Rosa's kids saw her lose weight and feel more energetic, they were inspired and excited to be healthier, too. *— Susan Dell*

"I started going to classes that my friend, Jovita, was teaching. She was teaching classes to try to help the people in our neighborhood get healthier. I started going because I had high blood pressure and high cholesterol. I didn't want to leave my home, but I got so depressed that I knew I had to do something. I had to be healthier.

One of the things I learned from Jovita's classes was to read labels. When I used to go shopping, I would just grab products without looking at what they contained. I didn't look at the ingredients or look to see how much sugar was in our foods. When I started reading the labels on drinks, I saw how much sugar there was in the things we were drinking.

My kids hated it when I stopped buying unhealthy foods and drinks. They were upset that I went to classes to learn about healthier things. They didn't like the changes, which made it hard. But I kept telling them, 'I'm doing this for your health. I'm doing this because it is healthier for you.'

It was amazing. Once my kids saw the changes I went through, they were on board with being healthier, too. For them, 100-percent fruit juices are like a party. They come home and yell, 'Yeah!' when they see this treat because we usually have water. They've learned to look at the labels, too, so if I don't take the time to look at the labels, they catch me and make sure we're drinking healthy drinks — if we aren't having water."

Angie
and her family

When Angie married a vegetarian, the amount of fruits and vegetables she and her son Tim ate at home increased. So did the amount of water they drank.

But Tim, like many kids whose parents have remarried, has two homes: His mom's and his dad's. So Angie faces a challenge that many parents do. She has had to make sure she's teaching her son to make healthy choices on his own.

Angie has also taught healthy habits to her three younger kids, whom she adopted with her new husband. For instance, they avoid sugary drinks, even juice, in favor of healthier choices. — *Susan Dell*

"Tim's dad has a lot of different habits than we have at my house. We have rules here in this house and sometimes they transfer to his dad's house and sometimes they don't. What I can do is help Tim to establish healthy habits so he'll make good choices when he's not at home. I've really tried to teach him to stay away from soda and drink plenty of water, which is tougher to do when he has access to it at his dad's house. Here, we don't have soda in the house. So I do what I can to encourage Tim to make the healthier choice.

I encourage him to stick with his healthy habits, no matter where he is. I encourage him to drink as much water as he can. Even if he has an occasional fruit drink or something else, I've told him to make sure he drinks enough water, too.

For our other three kids, we've dropped juice from our diet because it adds sugar without the benefit of an actual piece of fruit. Skim milk and water are my youngest children's primary beverages. Lemonade or diet root beer are treats served on occasion. As mom, I drink lots of water and encourage the kids to do the same. I'm teaching them that water is the most important thing they can drink every day."

4

EASY STEPS TO
be well
this month

1 Keep sugar-sweetened beverages out of the house. **Kids can't drink what isn't available to them**.

2 Drink **water** with every meal.

3 Choose **plain low-fat or fat-free milk** for your child instead of sweetened flavored milks.

4 Encourage your kids to **drink more water** than any other beverage by making water accessible and even tempting. **Get reusable bottles that are fun** for the kids to drink out of or add real fruit to flavor the water.

Important tips:
• Small steps can have a big impact.
• Choose one or two steps to begin each month.

Resources

PUBLICATION

Cool Waters
Brian Preston-Campbell

MOBILE APP

DrinkNow

ORGANIZATION

Healthy Beverages in Child Care
www.healthybeverages inchildcare.org

COMMUNITY

Your own water faucet

Eat Real Food,
Not Junk Food

I n the past 30 years, Americans have seen an increase in the proportion of calories our children obtain from fast food, convenience store food, and other foods eaten away from home. However, most of the calories we eat still come from home.

This is great news! It means we have so many opportunities to give our children the real food they need: fresh fruits and vegetables, lean meats, plenty of water, fat-free and low-fat dairy items, and high-fiber whole grains.

One way I've tried to do this is to really include my children in meals. When kids are involved in planning and preparing meals, they are more likely to eat what is on the table. They also enjoy doing things like "eating a rainbow" by eating different colored foods that only occur in nature. This makes it easier for them avoid foods with a lot of artificial colors, flavors, or preservatives. Kids who are repeatedly exposed to certain foods are more likely to try and like them. Food gives us all a chance to interact with our children and save time and money.

I have other tips that I try to share with parents who want to avoid junk foods. I don't buy unhealthy snacks like potato chips or candy bars. If my kids don't find those items in the house, then they won't be able to eat them. We eat healthy fruits that are tasty and sweet as a treat. And I involve the kids in cooking. The more involved your kids are, the more they will want to eat the healthy meals they helped create. *– Susan Dell*

Did **you** know

The average consumption of sweets and bakery desserts is about eight to 10 servings per week in 5- to 9-year-olds and 10- to 14-year-olds and six to eight servings per week in 15- to 19-year-olds.
American Heart Association

Nearly half of U.S. middle and high schools allow advertising of less healthy foods, which impacts students' ability to make healthy food choices.
Centers for Disease Control and Prevention

Jovita
and her family

Jovita's Chicago home used to have a trash can full of processed food wrappers and empty soda cans. Grain-based desserts, like cookies, cakes, pastries, and donuts, are a leading source of calories and a major source of saturated fat and added sugars in the diets of Americans of all ages, so it's not surprising that Jovita lost weight and lowered her cholesterol when she eliminated these foods from her diet. — *Susan Dell*

"My house is a 'no fry zone,' and I don't do 'whites' — no white flour or white sugar is used in our house. Since my kids eat what I serve them, they can't eat fried foods or sugar if I don't put them on the table.

What I do put on the table are healthy options. I keep clean fruit in a bowl on the kitchen table so it's easy to grab. I make a lot of healthy shakes with oatmeal, mangoes, and flaxseed so my kids have a quick, healthy breakfast. It takes more time to plan out meals in advance, but I do my shopping for the week at one time so I don't have to stop by a fast-food restaurant when I'm in a hurry. I've got food ready at home no matter when we need it. We've basically eliminated fast foods from our diets.

I serve whole-grain, high-fiber breads and cereals rather than refined grains. I look for 'whole grain' as the first ingredient on the food label and make at least half of our grain servings whole grain. I know that healthy habits are formed over time. We started with small changes and gradually changed many parts of our lives."

Andrea
and her family

A lot of people think the least healthy foods come from fast-food restaurants. Andrea's family in Tucson proves that even food made with some of the best intentions can have the worst effect on your overall health. Often, it's the high-fat foods we've loved since we were kids that have been leading to legacies of poor health, diabetes, and heart disease. — *Susan Dell*

"My family shows love through food. When we want to show joy, we make food. When we want to show concern, we make food. When we want to show anger or sorrow or happiness or whatever, we make food. And in my culture, we traditionally make a lot of food with a lot of lard: refried beans, tamales, and tortillas.

I had to figure out how to make traditional dishes in a healthy way. Then, I had to convince my aunts and older members of the family that I was actually helping them — not dishonoring them — by changing our long-standing recipes. They thought I was passing judgment on them for cooking with lard and complained when I tried to serve dishes like healthy pinto beans from my Crock-Pot instead of refried beans.

We now grow herbs and spices at our house so we have fresh ingredients for our recipes. We've learned that the fresh cilantro we grow at home is even more fragrant and full of flavor than the kind we can buy at the grocery store.

I taught my family that 'real food' is actually the food I'm now serving. We can taste the fresh vegetables and spices instead of the oils. The flavors of the peppers and marinades come through when the lean meats are grilled instead of fried. I know what I'm serving my whole family — no matter what we're celebrating or sharing — is healthy."

Rochelle
and her family

Preparing foods yourself is a great way to eat well, save money, and spend time together. Your children can get the nutrients they need from healthy dishes and learn to use the foods that are available to them at different times of the year. Rochelle's Philadelphia family is living proof of this. — *Susan Dell*

"I believe in doing things the natural way. The most important lesson I'm teaching my children is to eat pure foods from the earth.

I know that eating too many processed foods can lead to obesity in children. So, I'm committed to making sure my seven children all eat natural foods. There are no processed foods in our house.

We still have treats sometimes. When we make baked goods like brownies, I try to make the entire process a family event. One child measures multigrain flour, another measures the dark chocolate, and so on. I only use about half of the sugar called for in these types of recipes, and my children don't even notice. But we think of treats in a different way, too. Our treats are sweet and tasty, but they are still healthy. Seasonal fruits like apples in the fall and peaches in the summer are treats in our home.

We are creatures of the earth, so I'm trying to teach my kids to eat in a way that will keep them going strong for a lifetime."

4

EASY STEPS TO
be well
this month

1 During **snack times**, make sure you **have plenty of fruit, veggies**, and other healthy snacks on hand.

2 Don't be afraid to **ask for healthier options or cooking styles at restaurants**. Go ahead and order a grilled chicken breast instead of a fried one.

3 Rather than visiting a fast-food restaurant, **visit your local grocery store** and pick up some fresh or frozen produce and lean deli meats for lunch. Some stores also have nutritionists to teach you how to read labels or how to shop the perimeter of the store. It will **save** you **money, time, and calories**.

4 In any given week, aim to **eat more food at home**, rather than eating out or purchasing processed food from a bag or box.

Important tips:
• Small steps can have a big impact.
• Choose one or two steps to begin each month.

Resources

PUBLICATION

In Defense of Food: An Eater's Manifesto
Michael Pollan

MOBILE APP

Fast Chicken Meals

ORGANIZATION

Eat Real Food
www.myeatrealfood.org

COMMUNITY

Your local grocery store

Go Green:
Increase Fruits and Vegetables

ncorporating more fruits and vegetables into your family's diet sounds easy. But many families can't easily get to stores that sell fresh fruits and vegetable. And it can be even harder to get kids who aren't used to eating healthy items to try them. The proof is in the numbers: Only 20 percent of high school students report eating fruits or green vegetables five or more times a day.

It can be hard for parents to fill their children's stomachs with apples, grapes, broccoli, or green beans rather than fill them with junk food. And eating a serving of fruit or vegetables at each meal doesn't even meet the number of daily recommended servings. So how can parents get their kids to consume enough of these essential foods? Three Be Well families found innovative ways to accomplish their goal. – *Susan Dell*

Did **you** know?

Studies show that people who consume many foods and drinks with added sugar tend to consume more calories than people who consume fewer of these foods.
National Heart Lung and Blood Institute

Serve fat-free and low-fat dairy foods. From ages 1 to 8, children need two cups of milk or its equivalent each day. Children ages 9 to 18 need three cups.
American Heart Association

Cindy
and her family

Cindy made lifestyle changes for her family when she was diagnosed with Type 2 diabetes. Cindy had to replace the fast foods they often ate with appropriate portions of protein (for example, lean meats, soy, and eggs), dairy products, healthy starches (foods like whole grains and brown rice), and produce (fruits and vegetables). She also became a master at making healthy practices and food options part of every family celebration and holiday — times when it is easy to overindulge in fatty foods with low nutritional value.

The family now views fruits and vegetables as staples of their diets. This practice has been so successful at improving their health that the family has lost a combined 150 pounds. — *Susan Dell*

"When I was diagnosed with Type 2 diabetes, I knew that I'd need help from the whole family to make some drastic changes in our lifestyle. One of the easiest ways we could all be healthier was to incorporate more fruits and vegetables into our meals — and I don't mean fried vegetables or sugarcoated fruits.

At every meal we have 4 ounces of protein — which is about the size of a deck of cards — one starch, one serving of fruit, and all of the vegetables you want. We just had to try different foods to see which ones each of us likes and keep those foods as staples in our kitchen all of the time.

At dinner each night, the only extra foods on the table are vegetables. We dish out meats and starches at the stove. We eat less of those because the only second helpings available are the veggies. I never tell my kids they can't eat more vegetables."

Jamilia
and her family

In many cities, finding a store that stocks quality fruits and vegetables can be hard. Oakland, California, is no exception. Jamilia has limitless energy and a commitment to feeding her five children plenty of produce each day.

Eating healthy in inner-city Oakland can be hard, where — like so many cities — quality fresh fruits and veggies are in low supply. So Jamilia loads her crew onto a bus and travels across the city to farmers markets where she can afford the fresh foods she wants. The only additional cost for Jamilia is the time it takes to complete these trips. Realizing that so many families in her neighborhood also wanted to have access to healthier food options, Jamilia began working with her local schools and farmers to organize farmers markets closer to home. Because of Jamilia's efforts, other parents have the chance to increase the fruits and veggies in their own families' diets. — *Susan Dell*

"I try to teach my kids that they have the option to control what they put in their bodies. I tell mothers to involve their kids in the planning, shopping, and cooking so they'll eat more of the fruits and vegetables they should be eating but don't always want to. If you involve the kids, they'll at least try the fruits and veggies — at our house they have to try it many times before they can officially decide that they don't like the food.

When I tried to get the kids to eat broccoli, I had to serve it raw once and steamed once before we figured out the ways each of the five kids liked to eat it. Who cares if I have to cook some and leave some raw every time I serve it? As long as they are eating it, I'm happy.

I also add at least one vegetable or fruit to every meal. A lot of times I'll add veggies like peas or carrots into my pasta sauces or things like tuna casseroles. These changes weren't very hard, I just had to add the healthy ingredient into my family's favorites. It takes a little effort on my part, but it's my responsibility to give them healthy options."

Debra
and her family

We first met Debra in 2008 when she was dropping off bags of sugar snap peas to her daughter's summer camp class at the Harlem YMCA. For Debra, returning to the Y with more food after her daughter's friends begged her to bring more was a small sacrifice to make sure kids in her neighborhood were exposed to fruits and vegetables.

Debra told us that many of the neighborhood's children, including her own daughter, were hooked on greasy or processed foods. Kids weren't used to eating the healthy items, so they wouldn't even try them when offered. So the challenge became getting the kids to eat them without a fuss. — *Susan Dell*

"When I started trying to get my daughter, Giovanni, and the other neighborhood kids who eat with us every night, to try vegetables, I thought I'd never hear the end of it. They all complained that they didn't like vegetables, but they hadn't even tried most of them. So I figured the best way to get the kids to eat healthier foods was to make healthy foods more fun.

We do things like make obstacle courses for action figures out of broccoli 'trees' and cherry tomato 'rocks.' I let the kids decorate whole-wheat pancakes with faces. They use shredded carrots for hair, raisins for eyes, and bananas for the mouth.

Our favorite thing to do is to make 'food necklaces' instead of candy necklaces. We use thread and a needle to string things like blueberries, strawberries, carrots, and pieces of red peppers to make a necklace that we can tie around our necks and munch on them until they are empty. The kids can get at least one serving of fruits or vegetables out of one necklace.

My momma always told me not to play with my food. But I try to come up with new ways to make food fun — whatever it takes to get healthy foods in the little bodies I feed."

4

EASY STEPS TO
be well
this month

1 Remember, when fresh fruit isn't available, look for **frozen or canned fruits and veggies** without added salt or sugar. They hold the same terrific nutrient base and are reasonably priced.

2 Learn to **mix fruits and vegetables** into other foods. Add veggies to pasta sauces or casseroles.

3 Make fruits and vegetables **fun**. Try dressing up sandwiches with faces and smiles made from fruits and vegetables. **Low-fat dips** like low-fat peanut butter and light dressings are perfect for dipping veggies.

4 Bring kids shopping to **help select** the produce they want to enjoy each week. Challenge them to **try a different** fruit or vegetable each week along with their favorites.

Important tips:
• Small steps can have a big impact.
• Choose one or two steps to begin each month.

Resources

PUBLICATION

Ripe: A Fresh, Colorful Approach to Fruits and Vegetables
Cheryl Sternman

MOBILE APP

Vegetarian Recipes Cookbook

ORGANIZATION

Fruits & Veggies More Matters
www.fruitsandveggies
morematters.org

COMMUNITY

Your local farmers market

Limit All
Screen Time

Let's face it: Technology is an enormous part of all our lives. It's our business, but we also enjoy our mobile devices, computers, and TVs. As big of a part technology plays in our lives, it's still amazing to me that school-age children spend an average of 7.5 hours a day watching TV and using other electronics. This is simply too much of a good thing.

While our kids are looking at screens, it means they are just sitting there. They aren't getting the physical activitiy they need each day.

Children ages 6 and older need at least 60 minutes of moderate physical activity a day; grown-ups require at least 30 minutes each day. Excessive screen time leaves less time for active, creative play. It also exposes children to a lot of advertisements for unhealthy junk foods and fast foods.

The American Academy of Pediatrics recommends limiting a child's use of TV, movies, video, and computer games to no more than one or two hours a day. Too much screen time has been linked to obesity, showing children who watch more than two hours of TV a day are more likely to be overweight. It is also linked to irregular sleep patterns. The more TV children watch, the more likely they are to resist going to bed and to have trouble falling asleep.

Take a look at the following stories and see how other parents are limiting screen time and making sure their kids are getting enough quality sleep each night.
– Susan Dell

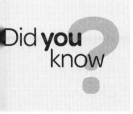

Angie
and her family

I love Angie's approach to limiting screen time. She avoids the usual trap of trying to entertain her kids with electronics and TV, instead making sure they're active every day, and that, whether they like team sports or not, they view themselves as athletes. Angie understands the benefit of technology and the Internet, so she allows her kids to have some screen time each day — but on a limited, reasonable basis.

She also practices what she preaches. Angie stays active by running and hiking on the trail near her home — which doesn't leave much time for this busy mom to sit in front of the television. — *Susan Dell*

"Turn off the TV. The kids and everybody else will find something else to do — and it usually involves doing more, sitting less.

My son Tim and I go biking on a trail near our house and go running together. Sometimes, he rides his bike beside me when I'm running, so we are doing something active together and not just sitting. We don't bond over TV.

My (oldest) son doesn't like team sports, but I told him that's OK. You can be active and be an athlete without being on a team. This is important because it means he isn't just sitting in front of a TV all day. I tell him that he can ride his bike or run or play with friends in the backyard, and that's what makes us athletes. It's not all about winning or taking home trophies. It's about having a wonderful, active experience and having fun.

I'm not sure what other parents do, but I tell my kids that it doesn't matter. It matters what we do in our house, and that means we're athletes. I don't care what activity they do, but they have to stay active and not sit around all day long. They don't have recess or P.E. class every day at school, so I've got to keep them away from the TV and active so they stay healthy."

David

and his family

David leads his son Jesse by his example. This carries over into David and Jesse's limited screen time. They've taken a different approach than Angie: They love team sports and use their love of baseball to keep them outside and busy. They spend time practicing pitching, lifting weights, or doing chores, always moving and laughing together and enjoying each other's company. They find each other much more entertaining than any TV show or video game. *— Susan Dell*

"Baseball is our connection between father and son. It's Jesse's favorite sport, so he plays in the fall and in the spring. I'm papa and coach. It's something we can do together and something that keeps him from just sitting and watching TV all day.

When baseball season is over in the summer, we do workouts every morning. Our workouts vary now. We do a full-body workout with light weights, calisthenics, and play ball. We practice correct posture with weights that aren't too heavy for a growing kid. Everything I've read says to keep the kids moving and build muscle tone by keeping the muscle growing at a nice, easy pace. I don't want him to lift weights that are too heavy and hurt himself. I've studied the right way to lift, and I've tried to teach that to Jesse.

Every child should have a healthy lifestyle.

We all need a little down time. But it is important that they stay active and exercise regularly. Two years ago, we'd do light calisthenics and walk and run each day. We did the mile loop around our neighborhood and kept track until we reached a total of 100 miles.

When we play basketball together, I will sometimes let Jesse rebound his own balls because he gets more exercise if he goes and gets them instead of me waiting to throw the ball back to him. Often I'll take him one-on-one.

When he wasn't in school, we'd go walk around museums or take hikes. We used to hike all the way around the lake in downtown Austin. We've always been an active family and it carries on. You won't see me sitting around doing nothing, so you won't see Jesse doing that either."

Guido

and his family

Guido is a Miami teenager who tells people that he fell in love with being active by swimming. I fell in love with Guido's commitment to staying active and replacing the time he spent watching TV with time spent swimming and playing with his friends. Even as a youth, he understands that cutting down on screen time is one of the easiest and most important things he can do to stay healthy. Guido is an inspiration to people of all ages. — *Susan Dell*

"I've tried to use my mouth to educate people and my body to stay active. I like to use the electronics that I've saved enough money to buy, but those things don't rule my life.

If I had to tell someone the first thing to do to get healthy, I'd tell them to do the simple things like cutting down on your TV time. That is something that anybody can do easily. That leads to being more active because you have to find things to fill your time and have fun.

I use my own experiences to educate other kids. I tell them that there are five things I do to stay healthy: 1) Cut down my TV time to one hour or less every day. 2) I eat fruits and vegetables with each meal. 3) I sleep 9 hours every night. 4) I stay active at least 60 minutes every day. 5) I try to be healthy with my friends. They are the 'fuel' that helps keep me going, and we teach each other.

I also stay away from the TV by swimming. It is my favorite sport. I started swimming in 2007 because my mom didn't know how to swim, and she wanted me to be able to. So she took me to the pool and made sure I learned. She thought it was important for my future, and it would also keep me busy and out of the house. She didn't want me to just sit around all day, either.

I started to learn how to swim and I fell in love with the sport. In 2008, I started competing. It's really fun being with your friends and swimming. After that, I was able to meet some milestones. I swim in the pool and in open water such as an ocean or lake. I've been working my way up through the distances, and last year, I swam my first 4K. I'm sure I'll swim my whole life."

4

EASY STEPS TO
be well
this month

1 **Limit use** of TV, movies, video, and computer games to no more than **one or two hours** a day.

2 Take TVs out of your children's bedrooms. **Set an example** and remove it from your/parent's bedroom, too.

3 Set a **kitchen timer to 60 minutes**. Whenever your child is watching TV or playing computer games, allow the time on the clock to elapse until his or her 60 minutes is up. This will help the **kids budget their own screen time** and help set clear expectations for the amount of time they should spend being sedentary without daily arguments.

4 Make the time for a **family activity** each day rather than making time for a TV show. Plan your life around **being physically active** rather than activities that require your family to sit still.

Important tips:
• Small steps can have a big impact.
• Choose one or two steps to begin each month.

Resources

PUBLICATION

Great Big Book of Children's Games: Over 450 Indoor & Outdoor Games for Kids (Ages 3 to 12) Debra Wise, Sandy Forrest (Illustrator)

MOBILE APP

Couch to 5K

ORGANIZATION

Kids Health
www.kidshealth.org/parent/positive/family/tv_habits.html

COMMUNITY

Playground at your local school

Get Moving

Children ages 6 and older need at least 60 minutes of physical activity a day, and adults need at least 30 minutes each day. Easier said than done.

Moving more and being more active are essential if you want to get healthier. And yet, there are many reasons that this is one of the hardest activities for families to do. Some families aren't in shape and feel the task of becoming active each day is too daunting. Others say they can't seem to find 60 minutes of free time to exercise or play. Whatever your reasons for lacking enough physical activity, there are affordable ways to keep moving that can fit into your busy schedule.

It's important for families to understand that small, easy steps can significantly increase our children's prospects for longer, healthier lives. My personal philosophy is "Fuel for Performance, and Train for Life." If we think of food as fuel, the right kind of fuel — or nutritious food — gives our children's bodies energy and their brains the nutrition they need to keep running. When their bodies are fueled through healthful eating habits — lots of water, healthy portion sizes, and all the green vegetables they want — they perform better, whether they're taking a test, playing music, painting a picture, or participating in a sporting event.

We've met some terrific parents who are incorporating these habits into their households in creative ways and building a lifestyle, not a quick-fix fitness or diet program. Striking a healthy balance between good nutrition and regular physical activity is absolutely crucial. *– Susan Dell*

Did **you** know?

Only one in three children are physically active each day.
National Association for Sport and Physical Education

Evidence shows that increasing physical education in schools can improve grades and test scores.
Centers for Disease Control and Prevention

Ashley
and her family

Ashley started running in her Houston-area community because of her dad. But now, her boys run with her, and she makes the activity a daily priority. Ashley surprises friends and neighbors by running with her boys each night. She was shocked at the reactions she got when she started telling her students and friends that they started running together as a family. They asked why she made her kids run. She couldn't believe that they didn't understand why she'd want the boys to be active! *– Susan Dell*

"You can't run right after you eat, and the kids can't wait until 8 p.m. to eat dinner. We usually eat dinner around 5:30 p.m. then run around 7 p.m. It gives us time to get homework done right after school and to play. It's also a lot cooler in the evening hours, so it's more comfortable when we run then. It's a lot easier to run in the cold than it is in the heat.

On the days that we're going to do something else in the evening, I take the boys running after school. If we go out on Friday or Saturday night, we run earlier in the day.

The running doesn't keep us from doing other things. Sometimes we play other games and run a little less. But we plan things around our running rather than plan our running around other things. We have to make it a priority.

We also push each other to be better. It is always good to have someone in your life who is pushing you and will keep encouraging you to achieve your goals and work harder. We're there to help each other when one of us doesn't feel like running each night.

When my boys race, they run together and cheer for each other. In running, they've joined forces, and I like to see that. They are both tired at night, they sleep well, and they are more athletic all around. Running and getting that energy out has also seemed to help improve my oldest son's grades and behavior in school."

Emilia
and her family

Emilia's son Sergio is her oldest child. He has been on the heavier side his entire life. She always knew that he was above the recommended weight for his age and size, so she started doing everything she could to keep him from continuing to gain weight. She started trying to keep him active and eating smaller portions. One of the biggest challenges Emilia faced was finding a way to get Sergio excited about physical activity. Luckily, she found a community-based program that he and her three other children love. — *Susan Dell*

"I had to have some help to keep Sergio busy and active. I found the Born to Run program at El Buen Samaritano in Austin, and he started running with his friends there every day during the week. Before we started coming to El Buen and being part of Born to Run, we would just eat and be at home. We weren't very active. Sergio would also complain that his skinnier, healthier friends could run faster and play soccer better. He got frustrated and expressed that something needed to change.

At first it was a struggle. I started by saying I was going so I thought they should come with me and participate in all the things there are to do at El Buen.

I knew that Sergio could use the Born to Run program to be more active. It took a lot of convincing to get him to go at first. I sat Sergio down and told him that just sitting, eating, and watching TV wasn't good for him. I remember the day he started to love Born to Run; he was so happy that day. He was thrilled when he discovered running, and he loved it! I was so thankful that he had finally found an activity he was interested in. Now he's the one who says, 'Let's go!' He's the one taking the initiative.

For him, he always thought he would have a hard time running and playing sports. But after he got involved with the programs at El Buen and started running regularly, he took off. He started playing soccer and being part of other activities that he never thought he'd be able to do. He also saw other results. His clothes started fitting differently. He started to want to be involved in more and more things. And, we've become much more active overall as a family. We play volleyball and go to the park."

Lakeysha
and her family

Lakeysha has three young kids: Elijah, Namaya, and Victor. She was in the military for eight years. There she learned that health, wellness, and fighting childhood obesity were worth her energy. She used to fight for the Navy. Now she fights for her kids' good health. — *Susan Dell*

"I hear every excuse in the book for why parents don't keep their kids physically active. I hear it all of the time. When I served in the military I found myself struggling through a lot of the exercise, too. But I try to point out the things I do to make sure I can keep my family active.

Proper planning is required to stay healthy. When I became a mom, I became aware of the dangers of different foods and the need for my kids to stay healthy. I realized there has to be some type of intervention to make sure they stay physically active.

In our house, as a healthy family, we go for walks every night, and on the weekends, we walk to the park and play for an hour. As an adult, I need to set the example, so my son and I run together. He doesn't just listen to me tell him he should be running, and he doesn't see me go and workout without him. We stay active and we do it together.

People have this notion that if you're in the military, you're healthy. That isn't entirely true. When I was in the Navy, I was over a fitness program for people who weren't in shape. That's where I learned a lot about how to teach people to be physically active every day who weren't used to being active. It was the same as teaching children the benefits of exercise and a healthy diet. It was that experience that helped me learn to break down exercise, study the ones that would be fun — not just a bunch of work — and how to teach kids about healthier lifestyles. One of the things I carried over from the military was the discipline. I've tried to teach my kids what I learned: If we want to do something, we can do it. We can set goals and achieve them. We think about the future and plan for that. I have to be disciplined enough to do what I'm asking my kids to do."

4

EASY STEPS TO
be well
this month

1 Take **small steps** to achieve 60 minutes a day within your normal routine. It doesn't have to be 60 consecutive minutes.

2 **Set goals.** Challenge each other to walk 100 miles over time by charting the total distance you walk each day. Once you reach 100 miles, do something to **celebrate**.

3 **Create walking challenges.** Wear pedometers and see who can walk the most steps each day.

4 Host **dance Saturdays** for 60 minutes each Saturday morning. Turn on your favorite music and dance with your kids! It's a fun way to get you all **moving and grooving**.

Important tips:
• Small steps can have a big impact.
• Choose one or two steps to begin each month.

Resources

PUBLICATION

365 Activities for Fitness, Food, and Fun for the Whole Family
Julia Sweet

MOBILE APP

I AM LOVE — Kids' Yoga Journey 2.0

ORGANIZATION

Let's Move
www.letsmove.gov

COMMUNITY

Walk around the block or mall

Get More
Sleep

There is so much research that has been done to prove that getting enough sleep is critical at every age. A lack of sleep can increase the risk of becoming overweight or obese and lead to other behavioral issues. Getting plenty of sleep each night can help your family members prevent childhood obesity and maintain a healthy weight.

Most children under the age of 5 need 11 hours or more of sleep per day. Children ages 5 to 10 require 10 hours of sleep or more per day. Children ages 10 to 18 need at least 9 hours of sleep per day.

There are many things you can do to help your kids get a good night's sleep. Creating a bedtime routine and going to bed at a time that allows your kids to get enough sleep will help. *– Susan Dell*

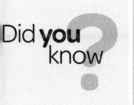

Did **you** know

People who report sleeping 5 hours a night are much more likely to become obese compared with people who sleep 7 to 8 hours a night.
National Heart Lung and Blood Institute

According to sleep experts, teens need at least 8.5 to 9.25 hours of sleep each night, compared to an average of 7 to 9 hours each night for most adults.
National Sleep Foundation

Donnie
and his family

Donnie's oldest son, 4-year-old Mateo, had trouble going to sleep and staying asleep. He was colicky and whiny all night. He just wasn't an innately good sleeper. After months of trying different approaches, Donnie and his wife found a nightly routine that helped relax their son and prepare him for a good night's sleep.

This family has made bedtime one of the most sacred parts of their day, always sticking to the routine that they know works. Now, both of Donnie's boys, Mateo and his youngest son, Austin, fall asleep and stay asleep for 12 hours every single night. — *Susan Dell*

"I love what we do every night — and we never miss a night. We know that sticking to our routine is important for the boys, and my wife and I enjoy it, too. She calls me 'The Closer' because I'm the one who consistently helps them end their day with what we do when they go to bed.

I've always enjoyed putting the boys to bed. Both of my sons have responded to us putting structure around our nightly routine. We're consistent with what time we put them to bed. Right after dinner, we have playtime then a bath. Right after our bath, we watch 20 minutes of a kids' TV show to let them wind down — it's really all the TV they watch in a day. We brush our teeth, get a drink of water, and then head into their bedroom to read books. We usually read 20 to 30 minutes, but they are usually asleep by the time I finish.

If they are still awake when I'm done reading, we say good night, turn out the lights, and they fall asleep easily. I usually sit outside the door and read for a few minutes to make sure they are down for the night and don't need anything.

The boys say that brushing their teeth is the favorite part of our nightly bedtime routine. I'm a big fan of the books."

Gaye
and her family

Gaye is a big believer in sleep and getting adequate rest. She knows how important sleep is to maintaining a strong body and immune function. With school-aged children, this is one controllable factor in helping to ward off unwanted colds and viruses and keep her kids healthy. — *Susan Dell*

"Last winter we dodged a number of 'sick bugs' — you know, the ones that seem to travel throughout the entire school! In years past, my daughter would have almost certainly caught all of them, but not last year. I attribute our success to several intentional practices, including eating more dark-colored vegetables and getting regular sleep. Here are some of the things that really seemed to help.

First, we established a regular bedtime. The key is to avoid the bedtime floating range and stick to a set time, so that the body is programmed to shut down.

Second, we have a consistent bedtime routine. In our house, bedtime prep begins with bath and brushing teeth and ends with reading. We like reading chapter books because it is so much fun to let the story unfold over several nights. It also helps to stop the 'but I'm not tired yet' comments, because she is anxious to get to the story.

Finally, we try to limit drinks past 7 p.m. to avoid sleep interruption. I know this is a hard one because of how most family schedules are these days, including ours. But these areas were affecting quality sleep because of frequent bathroom trips and bad dreams. In addition to getting to sleep, it's just as important to stay asleep. Some of the best benefits to adequate sleep are a bright mind and a positive attitude. I hope that these ideas help your family and remind us all that multiple factors contribute to good health."

Wendy

and her family

Wendy learned the impact that food could have on sleep patterns the hard way: She suffered from stomach issues that were worsened when she ate unhealthy foods. Medication didn't help her situation, but reducing her stress level and improving her diet led to a better night's rest once she fell asleep.

Wendy has tried to teach her daughters good sleep habits, too. She knows that so much of her daughters' mood, performance in school, and energy levels depend on the number of hours of sleep they get each night. – *Susan Dell*

"Food affected my health and sleep habits several years ago. My life was very hectic trying to be involved in the girls' schools and taking them to their activities. Each night, when I went to sleep, I had the need to throw up for a couple of hours. This definitely affected my quality of sleep. I decided to go to the doctor, and he determined that the cause was acid reflux. He prescribed medication and recommended that I come back.

The medication helped only a little. When I went back, he asked me if my life was stressful, and I said no. But I realized my life was hectic. He told me that I needed to slow down and change my eating habits: eat smaller meals, eliminate fatty and fried foods, and don't eat late at night.

After I made those changes to my diet, I have had very few incidents of acid reflux. This in turn has improved my sleep.

I feel that sleep is very important. I have read that sleep affects health, but I have seen firsthand that it affects behavior and attitude. I have had to be vigilant about my daughters' cellphones because it is surprising how many kids are up late on school nights socializing via Facebook and text messages. One of my children is a night owl, and I have found that structure and exercise help. By getting up early and being physically active during the day, it is easier for the body to wind down and be naturally tired at a more normal time."

4

EASY STEPS TO
be well
this month

1 Plan nighttime activities early so your kids **have plenty of time to get ready for bed** and allow for the recommended amount of sleep.

2 Help your child develop a **bedtime routine** and try to **stick to it.**

3 Encourage your kids to **use their beds for sleeping**, not watching TV or playing with electronics. You can limit screen time by **keeping electronics out of their bedrooms**.

4 **Avoid** large meals or heavy foods **before bedtime**.

Important tips:
• Small steps can have a big impact.
• Choose one or two steps to begin each month.

Resources

PUBLICATION

The Harvard Medical School Guide to a Good Night's Sleep
Lawrence Epstein, Steven Mardon

MOBILE APP

Sleepysound

ORGANIZATION

National Sleep Foundation
www.sleepfoundation.org

COMMUNITY

Your own bedroom

Make Friends
and Buddy Up

Nutrition and fitness buddies can help you become more health conscious and encourage you to stick to your routine. Research shows that this is even true for kids: They tend to eat better and be more physically active if their best friends are, too. It also shows that people may be more successful losing weight through physical activity when they have partners or buddies.

Buddies can be family members, friends, or co-workers. Find someone you enjoy spending time with and commit to being more active and practicing healthy habits. Ideally, you'll find someone who has similar goals as you so you can truly motivate and challenge each other.

Eating better and being active with a friend makes it more fun!
– *Susan Dell*

Did **you** know

Your chance of becoming obese increases 171 percent if a close friend is obese.
Behavioral Diabetes Institute

27 percent of young Americans are too overweight to serve in the U.S. military.
American Heart Association

Donnie
and his family

Donnie is a special education teacher from Boston whose own change in his habits motivated his longtime friends. The father of two young sons has learned how to turn his community into a walking trail for his entire family, using his legs to get him to and from the store, the park, and the riverfront. His positive attitude is contagious. — *Susan Dell*

"Getting into walking has been good for me, my family, and my friends. I started walking and changed my eating habits so much that I lost 54 pounds the first year! I kept track of how much I walked on a pedometer. Two miles here, two miles there — it all adds up.

It's good time for us to spend together as a family and do things outside the house. We walk to the supermarket, get our groceries, and head home. Once my son started getting more active and moving, we started exploring parks, visiting spray parks, and walking along the river. We have a beautiful river where we stop and feed the ducks and look at the frogs. Or we go 'off road' and climb rocks and trees.

I've found that walking has also helped me utilize parts of the city I never used before I was a parent. It's made me really appreciate where we live, which is good for my kids.

As a teacher, I started incorporating physical activity in my classroom because I saw the benefits for myself. And I try to be a role model to others. I have friends I walk with that I've grown up with since elementary school. One of my buddies lives five houses away, and we walk several times a month together.

The friends I recruited to walk with me have kids about the same age as mine, so we load the kids up in the strollers and walk to the park or somewhere in our city where the kids can play. At first, I was more into it than my friends, but they saw the benefits that walking had on me, and they got more excited about it. My buddy, Dave, will now wear a pedometer like I do, and we compete to see who can walk the most miles in a certain period of time.

It's great to spend that time walking with other dads because it also gives me a chance to talk about being a dad and share stories. I have two boys. Dave has two girls. We watch how our kids interact differently, and we're amused by the ways they are so different. It's great."

Stevon

and his family

Even though Stevon is the facilities coordinator at the Coleman Park Community Center in Nashville and has access to workout facilities, it is hard to find time for this busy dad of two girls to exercise regularly. Stevon relies on a group of friends who meet five mornings a week to work out and encourage each other. They know the others will be there to motivate them and challenge them. And they're all in better shape for it. Their children all know their dads workout every day and benefit from their healthy example. — *Susan Dell*

"I'm a former basketball player, but now working out is my sport. I meet a group of guys every day at 7:15 a.m. at the community center because it is an affordable place to work out in Nashville. It's less than a dollar a day for an individual to join and use the facilities.

Our workouts consist of 45 minutes of circuit training and laps around the track. We go full force. No rest. We work on every muscle group each time. It's a tough workout, but we pace ourselves and make sure we're safe. A 'challenging workout' can mean different things to different people, so it's important that we study and learn which exercises are best suited to our bodies and will help us achieve our goals.

A lot of my friends are former athletes. Lots of the guys in the gym every day are guys I've known for years. We've built a friendship, and we like to see each other healthy and in better shape. Other people in the gym are inspired, I think, because they see a group of guys who are trying to keep an athletic, healthy build and stay in shape. They see that we're doing it together. We respect each other and what the others are trying to accomplish. We're role models for each other and for the kids in our community."

Lakeysha

and her family

Lakeysha not only partners with friends and members of her church to stay active each week, she has partnered with her family to stay motivated and to keep one another accountable. Lakeysha knows that they'll all be more successful if they work together to lead healthier lives — and that means everyone wins! — *Susan Dell*

"When you find a buddy or partner, you can come together and keep each other accountable. I have a friend who has similar interests, and we keep each other in check. We both have families, so we can teach each other how to help our families be healthier.

I have taught her about fruits and vegetables and the importance of eating them every day. I've tried to teach her about where to get healthy foods and about little tricks to make sure our families are getting enough servings every day. For example, I've taught her how to store fruits and vegetables to keep them fresh. I've shown her the trick of keeping fruit on the kitchen table so they are visible, making it is easy for her family to grab. We also work together to create recipes that the family likes that are healthy, too.

She teaches me new things, too, like how to do a marathon because she is a triathlete. She's taken us hiking, and I'm showing her other ways to exercise. We keep each other accountable.

I think it is important for everyone to hook up with someone who is living a healthy life who can complement what you're doing on you own.

I think it is also important that you partner with your own family members to stay motivated. Try new activities together as a family. For my own family, I wanted to teach my kids about running and how to enjoy it. They didn't want to do it at first so I told them we can try running but also do other things they enjoyed, like swimming and skateboarding. They kept at the running and now we enjoy doing races together as a family."

4

EASY STEPS TO
be well
this month

1 **Find a buddy:** Eating better and being active with a friend makes it more **fun** and helps you stick to your goals.

2 **Challenge a friend to meet you** at the grocery store, your local park, trail, or even the mall (to walk) for a **healthy outing**.

3 Have a **backup plan** in case you're not able to meet with your partner.

4 **Let your children pick** an after-school sport or other physical activity. The more involved they are the **more fun** they will have!

Important tips:
• Small steps can have a big impact.
• Choose one or two steps to begin each month.

Resources

PUBLICATION

How to Be A Friend: A Guide to Making Friends and Keeping Them (Dino Life Guides for Families) Laurie Krasny Brown, Marc Brown (Illustrator)

MOBILE APP

FitnessFriend

ORGANIZATION

WebMD
www.webmd.com

COMMUNITY

Your neighborhood park

Go to **School**

Throughout the years, research has found that school-based programs that help kids "Fuel for Performance, and Train for Life" can significantly influence children's environment, behavior, and ability to succeed.

For example, Coordinated Approach to Child Health — or CATCH, a school-based program funded in Texas — is a terrific model for coordinated school health. The key to its success is its holistic approach. It combines nutrition education, healthy food options, a physical education program, and a family program to ensure healthy habits are continued at home.

CATCH has reached 2,500 elementary schools and 1 million children in Texas alone. Research has shown that CATCH can help to decrease obesity rates and increase the time kids are engaged in vigorous physical activity during P.E. class. Since it began, CATCH has expanded to other grade levels beyond elementary.

Over the years, we have found that school-based approaches to reduce childhood obesity are highly effective, and more parents should know about them and find a way to participate or champion them. For example, the Alliance for a Healthier Generation's Healthy Schools Program works in 14,000 schools across the country helping schools, at no cost to the school, adopt policies and practices that make healthy eating and physical activity the norm, not the exception, on school campuses. A recent evaluation of the program found that more than 80 percent of schools made positive improvements to help students eat better and move more. So without question, the model works.

Take a look at three stories of people doing those things already, and think of your own ways to get your family healthy. *– Susan Dell*

Did **you** know ?

One in three children born in 2000 are likely to develop Type 2 diabetes. The rate is even higher for children of color — nearly one in two Latinos and two in five African-Americans.
Centers for Disease Control and Prevention

P.E. is provided at only 3.8 percent of elementary schools, 7.9 percent of middle schools, and 2.1 percent of high schools.
Centers for Disease Control and Prevention

David
and his family

A few years ago, David decided to join a group of dads who volunteered at his son Jesse's middle school. The school wanted to attract male volunteers who could be role models to the kids and help supervise lunch. The students had access to a playground and activities they could use after lunch, but there were no teachers available to supervise the kids. The group of dads, called The Scottie Dads, have made a positive impact on all of the students and helped the kids at Lamar Middle School to be active. – *Susan Dell*

"The Scottie Dads are a group of men who come to my son's school and volunteer to supervise lunch and free playtime after the kids eat. I volunteered for it with nine other dads. We went through Partners in Education and received training from the school.

When the kids finish a nice healthy lunch, they get to go outside and play. We've got basketballs, volleyballs, soccer balls, Frisbees, and other games for the kids to play together, so they can be active during the school day. They don't have P.E. every day in their middle school, so we give the kids a chance to be social and active at the same time.

A lot of the kids will run or walk on the track together. The main thing is for them to keep moving, rather than just sitting there passing time. The majority of the kids really enjoy this.

The Scottie Dads were needed to help give the kids more of a male presence at the school and be an example to the kids. We have a limited number of male teachers, and even though our female teachers are great, we talked to a lot of kids who really liked having a dad there. We give the kids exposure to community members who aren't required to be there, but who care enough about the kids to be there.

I guess the kids see me there and see me as somewhat of a disciplinarian. But I also want to be an involved example to them as someone who was in the Marine Corps, as someone who works out every day, and as someone who cares about his kid and the other kids at the school."

Wendy

and her family

When Wendy's three daughters were young, she and her husband made the decision that Wendy would quit her job and stay at home as a full-time parent. This gave her time to get really involved in the girls' school and participate in organizations like PTA. Wendy took advantage of the opportunities she was given to share healthy tips and ideas with other parents and helped the P.E. teacher launch some creative campaigns at school. — *Susan Dell*

"Part of what I did for the PTA was to write the newsletter. I thought this was a great way to educate families about healthy habits. I looked on the Internet and at the school library for important information to share with families, then included it in each newsletter.

I worked with the P.E. teacher to develop games and activities that would teach the children about the benefits of healthy foods and exercise and try to get them to incorporate those things at home. I also created a challenge for the kids to try a different healthy food each week. In P.E. class, the students would identify the foods they had tried. It became a great way for them to encourage each other to try new foods.

As I reflect on my work encouraging healthy lifestyles, I see that my girls have different attitudes about this that are related to their ages.

In elementary school, it is cool for a parent to be involved. In middle school, I have found that they feel as if it is not cool for a parent to be involved, and kids seem to be very interested in junk food. In high school, it is once again OK to be involved, as long as they do not feel as if you are spying on them. They also become more independent in food and drink choices. Other kids seem to have more influence on their choices.

The attitudes again evolve in college when they are on their own as far as food choices go. This is where I believe that you will see the benefits of encouraging a healthy lifestyle early on. Once in college, they can begin to see the consequences of less exercise and poor food choices. I feel as if this is the time that attitudes and mindfulness toward a healthy lifestyle become more relevant. I'm glad my oldest daughter has the tools in which to make better choices."

Ashlyn
and her family

Ashlyn has been so successful at leading a healthy lifestyle, she now visits schools around New Orleans and shares her story. When she speaks to other kids, she shares the things that made her want to get healthy, stay healthy, and live a healthy lifestyle. She tries to drive home the point that, in the end, living a healthier life is what everyone should want to do. Ashlyn's using her voice and the school system to educate other kids for free. *— Susan Dell*

"I was talking with the school board because I wanted to find a way to introduce healthier habits at the schools. We came up with the idea of having a health rally.

We invited different speakers to come in and talk to the youth. We chose a school and had students from every school in Jefferson Parish attend. We gave them healthy snacks, we taught exercises, and we had booths that focused on different healthy habits. We also taught games that they could do to help them stay active. It was a really big hit, and it has turned into an annual event.

The school board is very into promoting health. They are dedicated to incorporating healthy activities and healthy habits at the school.

Teachers are also great with it. My P.E. coach took the programs we started and ran with them. We've been working together to educate the teachers about healthy living and coming up with activities that they can do together within the school. They now have yoga and other activities that they can do after school, so the teachers — our role models — can be healthier and more active, too.

We've seen a lot of great changes in the past few years. We've changed the vending machines. Our school started serving salads at lunch and offering different physical activities for the students to do when they finish eating. One day we'll have yoga, one day we'll have circuit training, and one day we'll have another different group activity. I'm really proud of our school and the work our school board and teachers have done to help our students be healthier. We all needed it!"

4

EASY STEPS TO
be well
this month

1 Visit **www.healthiergeneration.org** and **enroll your school** in the Alliance for a Healthier Generation's Healthy Schools Program.

2 Talk to your child's P.E. or health teacher about ways you can **volunteer at the school** and **help kids learn healthy habits**.

3 Go to your local **farmers market** or grocery store and let children pick out new foods to try.

4 **Pack a fruit or vegetable** in your child's lunch or for a snack.

Important tips:
• Small steps can have a big impact.
• Choose one or two steps to begin each month.

Resources

PUBLICATION

Free for All: Fixing School Food in America
Janet Poppendieck

MOBILE APP

School Snacks

ORGANIZATION

YMCA
www.ymca.net

COMMUNITY

Your child's school

MONTH 12

Pass It On:
Spark a Community Effort

There is a need for individual leaders, both adults and kids like Ashlyn and Guido, to step up and collaborate in their communities and inspire people to take the small, simple steps to a healthier lifestyle. You'll be surprised at what you can accomplish. As I learned about the kids in this book, it reminded me of my nephews Ryan and Blake who started Camp SPARK a few years ago, and my son Zachary who has since partnered with them to help expand Camp SPARK across the country. The Camp SPARK (Strong Powerful Athletic Rockin' Kids) mission is to get kids physically active while learning about good sportsmanship. What started as a few kids gathering for a week has now turned into summer day camps that provide a unique camp experience for hundreds of kids.

Zachary ran Camp SPARK this summer in Austin for more than 80 boys between the ages of 5 and 12. Zachary's friend Ethan ran Camp SPARK in California, specifically for underprivileged kids. Ryan and Blake ran Dallas Camp SPARK in their own home for two years, but this past summer, they asked to use their school gym and fields and were able to hold a much bigger camp there. They also worked with their friend Morgan to open up the first Camp SPARK for girls. Ryan, Blake, and Zachary also help arrange for sponsors to help those campers who can't otherwise afford to go to camp.

My hope is that you'll also find the motivation within yourself, your children, and your community to take that first step to ensure a healthy future for our next generation.

It's up to us to be the voice of our children, to demand changes in policy, our communities, and our schools, and to teach our children the importance of good nutrition and physical activity. Now go forth, be the difference, and be well! — *Susan Dell*

Stevon

and his family

Stevon is an athlete in every sense of the word, but he's also a father, husband, and community innovator. He attended college at Southern Mississippi and majored in sports management. He had great internships with the NBA developmental league, as well as the Baltimore Ravens. They were great high-profile jobs, but he felt his mission in life needed to be to give back to the community. So he went to Nashville, Tennessee, got involved in the Metro Parks Department, and started programs that are improving the lives of hundreds of kids each year. — *Susan Dell*

"I came to the Coleman Community Center for the first time in 2003. We didn't have many kids who could take advantage of the center because the intersection where we're located is the busiest one in Nashville, and the neighborhood has a lot of gang violence. It wasn't safe for the kids to walk here, and a lot of them didn't have transportation. I set out on a mission to grow that program.

I knew I needed to work with the schools on a solution, but I also knew I needed help. I needed to get support from state representatives, city councilmen, and community leaders so they could help open doors for me and get me in front of the principals at the schools in Nashville.

When I shared my plans for a free after-school program, the principals, government officials, and business leaders were all on board. They were sold on my idea of creating a program that enriched the kids' lives every day and gave them a safe place to go.

The biggest hurdle we had to cross was transportation. So I went in front of the school board and shared our plan — to have school busses drop the kids off at the community center like a regular bus stop. We agreed to meet the buses and sign the kids in each day, and their parents would sign them out at night. The plan was approved unanimously.

We went from 10 to 15 kids at the center to 125 kids in our after-school program. It's a great sound to hear them every afternoon. It's one of my biggest accomplishments."

Guido

and his family

Guido is part of the Alliance for a Healthier Generation's Youth Advisory Board, a group of 20 students chosen by the Alliance to be advocates for good health. Their goal is to help kids across the country get and stay healthier. Guido said his goal is to spread the health bug throughout his hometown of Miami and across the United States. — *Susan Dell*

"It all started when I attended a speech that President Bill Clinton gave in our school district. I got to go because I was part of the running club at my old school, North Beach Elementary. We went to the speech, and there he said that this generation would be the first to die younger than our parents. I was really concerned when I heard this and wanted to do whatever I could to help.

A few weeks later, some people from the Alliance for a Healthier Generation, which was founded by the American Heart Association and the William J. Clinton Foundation, came to my school.

My P.E. teacher told the Alliance how much President Clinton's speech impacted me and that I wanted to do whatever I could to help kids from dying before their parents. I was recommended for the Youth Advisory Board.

I try to use my voice for good. I have visited other schools to try to teach kids what they can do to live longer than their parents. Recently, I was able to visit a health and career day at another school and go from class to class and talk to kids about how they can stay healthy and what they can do to spread that message to their friends as well.

At my school, they opened up a salad bar. I made a commitment to eat salad at least two times a week, every Tuesday and Thursday. I would go and eat from the salad bar when it was available. Once my friends saw me eating salads, they said, 'Wow. He's actually doing that. He's eating salad, and it doesn't look too bad. I think I'll try that, too.' So a lot of people from North Beach Elementary started eating the salads."

Xinia
and her family

As a mother, Xinia believes it is her job to make sure her children have every chance in life. That begins with health. I can't think of a better gift to give your children than strong bodies and minds. — *Susan Dell*

"When my kids needed a safe place to play and exercise, a group of moms started a campaign to revamp the park in our neighborhood. We raised $400,000 for the project by asking for state funding and getting the support of our local politicians. The park was once dilapidated, but now it has a new playground and a grassy area for children to play baseball and soccer. It's all because a group of moms wanted to see changes happen in our neighborhood.

I also wanted to improve the foods the kids in our neighborhood had access to. I was unhappy when I saw how many unhealthy items were on the menus at the local restaurants near our home. So I called and visited the businesses to ask owners and chefs to serve healthier foods instead of things that were fried. It was hard not to be frustrated when so many people slammed the door in my face. I was surprised when some of them actually started to listen.

Now some of those restaurants are serving fruit cups, whole-wheat sandwiches, lean turkey, chicken, and low-fat menu options. Many of them now serve a whole list of healthy options.

The experiences I've had prepared me to work with the University of San Diego State Foundation and the Network for a Healthier California to hold community seminars on nutrition, exercise, and healthy living. It's a great way for me to help other moms.

Mothers need to ask for what they need for their children. It doesn't hurt to have your voice heard. It can help everyone if you speak up."

4

EASY STEPS TO
be well
this month

1 **Visit** with your neighbors and determine the few things that could be done in your **community** to get people moving more in the neighborhood. **Work together** to write your city's leaders to bring about change.

2 Start your own **Be Well Walk**. Organize a group of friends and neighbors to walk with you and make their own **commitment to being well**. Share your story on Facebook.com/bewellbook for a free water bottle.

3 **Survey** your neighbors and identify the things your **community needs** to help families live healthier. Do you need more walking trails or more playgrounds? Take your list to community leaders and get the ball rolling toward **positive changes**.

4 Identify free or affordable resources available in your community, then share your list with your friends and neighbors.

Important tips:
• Small steps can have a big impact.
• Choose one or two steps to begin each month.

Resources

PUBLICATION — *The Good Food Revolution*
Will Allen, Charles Wilson

MOBILE APP — Free Deck Workout

ORGANIZATION — Kaboom!
www.kaboom.org

COMMUNITY — Your local city hall

Reflect
and **Re-plan**

I n all of our work to prevent childhood obesity by addressing these various touch points, we've learned a few things. We don't have all the answers, but steady progress is being made, and now we have a compass for approaches that work to address those touch points in our children's day. Whether you are a parent, teacher, community member, or policy maker, you have significant power to shape a healthy future for our children.

My challenge to you is this: I encourage you to become a champion for instilling healthy habits in our next generation and consider ways to help them "Fuel for Performance, and Train for Life." Whether it's creating a healthy school environment, developing a community where it is safe to play and healthy options are available, or affecting the lives of your own children at home, you can help your community's children live healthy, active lives.

Once you've started incorporating healthy habits in your home, stop and evaluate the progress you've made. Ask yourself: What have I done well? What can I do differently? Go find more information. Seek help and guidance from new resources. Find more buddies. Try new foods and physical activities that you've never tried before.

Any progress is good progress, but we can all improve our lifestyles and be healthier. Don't get frustrated. Like some of the families in this book have done, when you stumble on the road to a healthier lifestyle, re-evaluate, re-group, and re-plan your approach and get back on track.

I know you and your family will be healthier because you did. *– Susan Dell*

Did **you** know

40 percent of every dollar spent on food is spent on food prepared outside the home.
United States Department of Agriculture

Only 27 percent of Americans eat vegetables three or four times per day.
United States Department of Agriculture

Cindy
and her family

Cindy's family once lost a combined 150 pounds, but lifestyle and job changes have made it more difficult for the family to maintain healthy weights over time. This is a common occurrence among growing families. But Cindy and her family re-evaluated their habits and are planning for a healthier year ahead.
– Susan Dell

"This year has been a trying time for our oldest son, Austin. He started at a new school, and the stress of it has been a challenge. He fell off his wagon and put some weight back on.

I was recently admitted to the hospital with stroke-like symptoms. Thankfully, it turned out only to be Bell's palsy, but I have nerve involvement, and it's very painful. My doctor said it is probably due to stress. I've been working the midnight shifts at the hospital for the past two years, and my body finally decided it didn't like it. It's amazing what stress and an unhealthy lifestyle will do to you.

Every family that has children who are overweight struggles with the same things. You think that they'll grow out of it. Unfortunately, this isn't true, and the harder their hearts have to work to move the weight, the less wonderful time on this earth you'll have with them.

I've had so many parents face the same challenges as me. We agree you have to lead by example, no matter how hard it is. The kids have to come first.

Every new day is a challenge. We've had to create new routines to fit around our busy schedule. I've been preparing sandwiches to have handy for when we're on the run, and we've tried new frozen fruits for treats.

Right now we also try to walk, walk, walk. It's free, and it's a great time to spend with the kids. It's amazing what they'll talk about on our walks! This summer, we are challenging the kids to walk 100 miles. They have to walk our street a total of two miles, so 50 times up and down our street will equal 100 miles.

There are so many wonderful, loving moms out there to learn from, too. Kids don't come with instructions, and we can all learn from each other."

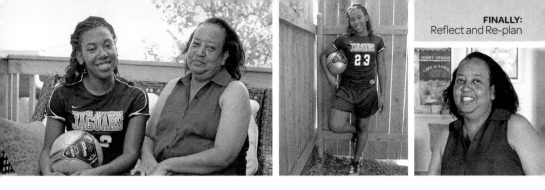

Ashlyn

and her family

Ashlyn is getting ready to go off to college, where she knows she'll be tempted by new things, and where it will be harder to get plenty of physical activity. She knows she'll have to keep watching what she eats and make a conscious effort to stay active. — *Susan Dell*

"When I enter college, I want to keep raising awareness about childhood obesity and healthy lifestyles, in general. I still want to volunteer and start up some clubs or a wellness council at the university. I've seen those work so well in high schools, so I'd like to see the same things happen where I'll spend the next four years.

I first cut out soft drinks to get healthier. Looking back on my habits, I'll keep going with that. It was a huge improvement. I never realized how many calories and bad things were in soft drinks and other sweetened beverages. I'm going to keep drinking water.

Right now, I would change my love for sweets. I love sweets, pastries, and things like that. It is so hard for me to stay away from those things, but that is something I'm really going to try to focus on now. I know they aren't good for me, so I need to limit those foods in my diet. Maybe I'll allow myself a treat every once in a while.

For exercise, I have sports teams that I'm part of right now, but I'm going to have to stay active in college when I leave home. I have practice every day now for track or soccer or cheerleading, but I won't have that at college.

When I get to school, I'm hoping to try out for a sports team or intramural team to stay active. If I don't make one of those teams, I'm planning on using the school's gym to work out and stay fit."

Angie
and her family

Angie is fortunate — in so many ways. But Angie probably faces the same challenges as any mom with multiple kids. She has a healthy weight teenage boy who eats as much as two grown men, a skinny 8-year-old boy who eats almost as much as the teenager, a 7-year-old girl who has a different body type than the boys, and a healthy weight 6-year-old boy who eats normal amounts for a little guy. And yet, Angie has learned to adjust her expectations and the lessons that she's teaching each of them to ensure they are all healthy and happy.
— *Susan Dell*

"Having a daughter has been interesting. Like me and her brothers, she loves food, but she tends to overeat. I've had to explain that we don't need to eat as much as the boys and her dad. Because I'm in this situation with her, I think it made it easier for her to accept. I want her to think 'healthy,' not 'skinny' or 'fat.' So we talk about portions and number of helpings.

I try to model the behavior I want to see in my children: healthy weight, lots of activity, a good attitude toward food, and everything in moderation. In our house, this also means we don't deprive ourselves of treats. I also make sure we have fruits and veggies, healthy grains, lean meats, and low-fat dairy for meals and snacks.

They're adventurous eaters, and I have a book of their favorite meals. They yell, 'Put it in the book, Mom,' when they love a food. Cracks me up! It's one of the ways I'm creating some new traditions for them. So much of family life and history is based on food and meals. When they're older and even after I'm gone, they'll have a book of all the favorite meals we shared."

4

EASY STEPS TO
be well
this month

1 **Take the stairs** instead of the elevator at work.

2 Try to keep **TVs out of your bedroom** and your children's bedrooms.

3 Hate broccoli? Try **preparing it different** ways to see if your taste buds prefer roasted over steamed.

4 Visit a grocery store and purchase a **healthy ready-made** sandwich or take a trip to the salad bar.

Important tips:
• Small steps can have a big impact.
• Choose one or two steps to begin each month.

Resources

PUBLICATION

*Plan It, Don't Panic:
Everything You Need to
Successfully Create and Use
a Meal Plan*
Stephanie Langford

MOBILE APP

Food Diary calorie counter

ORGANIZATION

MayoClinic
www.mayoclinic.com/health/
childhood-obesity

**IN YOUR
COMMUNITY**

Start a new journal

Acknowledgements

t took many talented and dedicated people to put *A Year of Being Well: Messages From Families on Living Healthier Lives* in the hands of families across the country. I'm honored that 20 exceptional families were willing to share their stories and give others the opportunity to benefit from their good examples. I extend my sincerest thanks to each member of those families and applaud you for the efforts you make for your families every single day.

I'm grateful to our partner on this project, the Alliance for a Healthier Generation and its founding partners, the American Heart Association and the William J. Clinton Foundation. Special thanks goes to Ginny Erlich, Sarah Hustoles, Megan McIntyre, and Kimberly Perry at the Alliance for a Healthier Generation.

The idea of the Be Well books was born in 2009, but it took the work of some talented people to bring the stories of each family to life. Thank you, Janet Mountain, Megan Matthews, Dr. Aliya Esmail Hussaini, and staff members at the Michael & Susan Dell Foundation, and Angela Austin and Renee Austin at Weber Shandwick.

The families that you read about in this book were selected from thousands of inspirational stories submitted by individuals and organizations across the U.S. Thank you to everyone who nominated such deserving families.

I'm appreciative of our friends at American Airlines Publishing, including KariAnne Harmon, J.R. Arebalo, Erica Espiritu, Casey Casteel, Jennifer Norris, and Brian Keagy for their counsel throughout the project.

Finally, thank you for reading *A Year of Being Well* and for taking the initiative to help your families lead healthier lives.

— Susan Dell

Notes

Notes

A Year of
Being Well

Narrated by Susan Dell

Messages from Families on Living Healthier Lives

BeWellBook.org

Table of Contents

Introduction

A*Year of Being Well: Messages from Families on Living Healthier Lives* is meant to be a guide for you as you set out on a journey toward healthier living. By beginning your year of being well, you've taken the first step toward a healthier lifestyle. The materials in this discussion guide are meant to help you succeed in your journey and spark discussion among your family or a group of friends, relatives, or community members. I challenge you to start your own group and work toward being well together.

Find a group of co-workers, friends, or community members who share your desire to lead a healthier life and instill healthy habits in your family. Then get free copies of *A Year of Being Well: Messages from Families on Living Healthier Lives* at www.bewellbook.org.

Meet regularly and discuss each month's healthy habits. Talk about the successes and challenges you've had. Discuss ways you can continue to develop those healthy habits. Share stories and resources. Learn from each other.

In this discussion guide, you'll find some tools you'll need to host an effective group, but you should find a structure that works best for your crowd. You can also find more information and resources at www.bewellbook.org.

Good luck and be well! — *Susan Dell*

Tips for the Facilitator:

- Take time to make introductions to get the conversation started. Any one of the following should help to get things going:
  — Ask each person the question, "Did you like the chapter?" during introductions.
  — Ask each person which healthy habit they focused on in the past month. (Reference the questions in the Recap section for each month within the discussion guide.)
- As a facilitator, it's your job to keep the discussion going.
  — Start with a recap of last month. Or if it's your first month, begin the discussion with where everyone is starting at with their family.
  — Use the questions in each month's For Your Discussion section to guide your conversation.
  — Ask others for their unique action steps that they want to share with the group.
- But most important, make sure everyone has an opportunity to share stories and resources. Learn from each other!
- Share important tips.
  — Small steps can have a big impact.
  — Choose one or two Easy Steps to Be Well to tackle each month. Don't overwhelm yourself.

Purpose:

To engage parents, teachers, and community members in discussions regarding their personal experiences and thoughts about *A Year of Being Well.*

When:

Schedule a regular meeting time for at least one gathering per month.

How to Start:

- Send out an email or letter of invitation to join your discussion group. Invite people you know or post a flier at your local community center, church, or school. Six to eight people per group is a good size, so everyone has a chance to talk.
- Order copies of *A Year of Being Well* and the discussion guide or download extra copies of the discussion guide at www.bewellbook.org.
- Set a time for your first meeting.
- Find a location for the initial meeting. If you feel comfortable inviting people into your home, you can have at least the first meeting at your home if you have enough room. Otherwise, free space can often be reserved at community centers, libraries, churches, or schools.
- If you call the first meeting, you can facilitate the first discussion. Agree within the group to rotate the facilitator role. The facilitator helps to keep the discussion on track, to educate members of the group, and motivate and inspire them to talk about their own experiences and ideas.
- Once the group is convened, introduce yourselves and facilitate an open and casual — but organized — discussion.
- Review the chapter of the month together.
- Participants will discuss the chapter for the month and talk with each other about what they have read and how it may or may not change their behavior regarding their child's or their own healthy habits. You can use the suggested questions and discussion topics in this guide to generate discussion if necessary.
- Participants should be encouraged to participate at their own level of comfort.
- Set a regular meeting time and reconvene. And remember to read the discussion meeting chapter just before your next discussion group.

1

Get
Started

Let's begin by talking about where you're starting at with your family.
- What healthy habits have you incorporated in your home in the past? Do you still practice those habits? If not, what made you stop?
- What are some common roadblocks people face on their journeys toward wellness?
- Share your reasons for joining the discussion group.
- In what ways have you succeeded in instilling healthy habits in your home? What healthy habits does your family have right now?

Healthy Habit of the Month

This month is all about taking your first steps on your journey toward a healthier lifestyle! Everyone has to start somewhere, but it always seems like starting something new is the hardest part.

With the frightening high obesity rates in the U.S., obesity isn't a problem that can be solved overnight. That's why we suggest incorporating one healthy habit, then adding a new habit each month for a year. This will give you time to master a healthy habit before adding a new one and help keep you from getting overwhelmed.

There's no right or wrong answer to where to begin incorporating healthy habits. *A Year of Being Well* is meant to be a suggestion guide to help you get on your way to good health. But it is critical that you think about your family's lifestyle and in-corporate changes — at the right time and pace — in ways that will increase your chances for success.

You'll see that the families in the book all started making changes at various times for various reasons. They live in different cities, they are from different ethnic backgrounds, and they faced different challenges when trying to lead healthier lives in their different communities. But they all started from the same place as you: the beginning.

For Your Discussion
- Who did you relate to the most: Jamilia, Sonora, or Gaye?
- What did you do last month to get started toward leading a healthy lifestyle?
- How did your family respond when you told them you wanted to start leading a healthier life? Were they excited, skeptical, or unhappy?
- What were some of the challenges you faced last month?

- What successes did you have last month?
- How has your family responded in the past if you've tried to incorporate new foods into their diet, increase the amount of physical activity they get, or encourage them to get enough sleep?
- Now that you're on your way to better health, what ideas would you share with others to make getting started easier for them?

More of This Month's Easy Steps to Be Well
- Buy a notebook or journal so you can track your food and activity or find a free online tracker like SuperTracker at www.supertracker.usda.gov. Start with keeping your journal for a week, then reflect on what areas of your diet and physical activities you need to improve.
- Have a family meeting and make a plan to implement healthy habits.
- Get organized to put your new healthy habits into place.
- Take an inventory of your habits so you can figure out what your triggers for bad habits are.
- If you pass fast-food restaurants on your way home, take a different route so you aren't tempted by fast foods.
- Make a shopping list and write down your healthy living goals each week.

More of This Month's Resources
- **Publication**: *Drop Dead Healthy*, A.J. Jacobs
- **Mobile app**: Lose It!
- **Organization**: Mission: Healthy Living, www.missionhealthyliving.org
- **In my community**: Your community health clinic

Notes

Get Smarter

RECAP OF LAST MONTH
- What Easy Steps to Be Well have you incorporated in your home in the past month?
- What were some of the challenges you faced in getting started?
- What tips can you share with others who are also trying to get started on leading healthier lives?

Healthy Habit of the Month
For years it's been said that knowledge is power. By understanding the health risks of an unhealthy lifestyle and ways to incorporate healthy habits, you can prepare to improve the overall health of your family.

We must all be students and utilize the many resources available to learn what it takes to be healthy. Finding information is easy. There are many publications, organizations, and free resources available in every community, on the Internet, and even on mobile phone applications.

Take a look at the ways families in *Being Well: Messages from Families on Living Healthier Lives* got smarter and started living better.

For Your Discussion
- Who in the book did you relate to the most: Jovita, Ashlyn, or Gaye?
- What information do you need at this point in your journey toward better health?
- Where will you go for additional information on living healthier?
- Are there people in your life who can offer advice or ideas to help you? If so, who can you contact?
- What free resources are available in your community?
- Where will you go to find additional information and resources?

More of This Month's Easy Steps to Be Well
- Learn how to read labels.
- Explore mobile apps that will help you track your progress.
- Get smart about what exercises burn the most calories.
- Figure out your ideal caloric intake based on your age, height, weight, and activity levels using an online resource and plan your meals and snacks to fit within your range.
- Start doing physical activities you enjoy. If you hate running, go for a swim. Your fitness plan is only as effective as the enjoyment it brings you.

More of This Month's Resources
- **Publication**: *The American Dietetic Association Guide to Healthy Eating for Kids: How Your Children Can Eat Smart from Five to Twelve*, ADA, Jodie Shield M.Ed. R.D, Mary Catherine Mullen M.S. R.D
- **Mobile app**: Healthy Grocery Lists & Food Scanner
- **Organization**: Meal Planning Made Simple, www.mealsmatter.org
- **In my community**: Your local public library

Notes

MONTH 3
Lead by Example

RECAP OF LAST MONTH
- What resources did you use to get smarter about healthy lifestyles last month?
- Are there resources that you found helpful?
- Where do you recommend others visit for more information on living healthier lives?
- What are some of the things you learned last month?

Healthy Habit of the Month
Leaders come in all shapes and sizes, ages, and races. Someone in your home must assume the role as leader and start the process of getting healthy or continue being an example for others.

People learn best through the examples of others, so it is important that as parents and role models we demonstrate good habits for our children. Kids will do what they see adults do. If we simply preach about instilling healthy habits but we don't practice good habits ourselves, we'll never succeed in helping kids eat better, get more sleep, or get more physical activity.

For Your Discussion
- Who in the book did you relate to the most: Ashley, Cindy, or Lakeysha?
- What behavior can you model for your family this month?
- Do you know someone who leads a healthy lifestyle? Who else can be an example for your family?
- How can your child be a leader at home this month?
- What else can you do to be a good example for your kids?

More of This Month's Easy Steps to Be Well
- Organize a block party or neighborhood meeting.
- Start a Facebook page or a poster board chart for your friends and family so you can all track your success together.
- Start a healthy progressive dinner in your neighborhood to help your friends and neighbors sample healthy foods.
- Get your family involved in the meal planning process. Ask each member to suggest a healthy recipe they want to try.

More of This Month's Resources
- **Publication**: *Women's Home Workout Bible*, Brad Schoenfeld
- **Mobile app**: Nike+ Running
- **Organization**: American Health and Fitness Alliance, www.health-fitness.org
- **In my community**: Your community center

Notes

4 **Drop** Liquid Calories

RECAP OF LAST MONTH
• How were you a role model for your family last month?
• Who else did you look to for help?
• How was your child a leader at home last month?
• What could you have done better? What bad habits did your kids see from you?
• How will you continue to be a good example for your kids?

Healthy Habit of the Month
Consuming sugar-sweetened beverages is often associated with obesity and adds more sugar in our children's daily diet than any other food. Replacing sports drinks, soda, and other sugary drinks and limiting your consumption of 100-percent fruit juice are effective ways to start the journey to healthier behaviors in kids and adults.

The Centers for Disease Control and Prevention has reported that on a typical day, 80 percent of youth drink sugary drinks, which are full of "empty calories."

Calories in drinks are not hidden (they're listed on the Nutrition Facts label), but many people don't realize how many calories beverages can add to their daily caloric intake. Check the chart in this section to estimate how many calories you typically take in from beverages.

For Your Discussion
• Who did you relate to most: Sonora, Rosa, or Angie?
• What sugar-sweetened beverages do you often have in your home?
• What beverages can you offer your kids that are healthier options?
• How will you replace the sugar-sweetened beverages in your child's diet?

More of This Month's Easy Steps to Be Well
• Avoid energy drinks that are high in sodium and sugar. The American Academy of Pediatrics concluded that energy drinks are never a good choice for children and adolescents and should be avoided.
• Remove all of the soda from your home. These are all sources of empty calories, and they

dehydrate you, too.
• Invest in water bottles so water becomes the easy choice for on the go. You'll stay hydrated and be much less likely to buy sugary beverages.
• Try juicing so you can get 100-percent juice for a healthy snack or beverage.
• Try some calorie-free beverage mixes to add some different flavors to your water.

More of This Month's Resources
• **Publication**: *You're Not Sick, You're Thirsty!*, F. Batmanghelidj
• **Mobile app**: Drink More Water
• **Organization**: National Milk Producers Federation, www.nmpf.org
• **In my community**: Your own water faucet

Type of Beverage	Calories in 12 ounces	Calories in 20 ounces
Fruit punch	192	320
100% apple juice	192	300
100% orange juice	168	280
Lemonade	168	280
Regular lemon/lime soda	148	247
Regular cola	136	227
Sweetened lemon iced tea (bottled)	135	225
Sports drink	99	165
Unsweetened iced tea	2	3
Diet soda (with aspartame)	0*	0*
Carbonated water (unsweetened)	0	0
Water	0	0

*Some diet soft drinks can contain a small number of calories that are not listed on the Nutrition Facts label. USDA National Nutrient Database for Standard Reference

Notes

5

Eat Real Food,
Not Junk Food

RECAP OF LAST MONTH
- What sugar-sweetened beverages did you reduce from your diet last month?
- Are there other new beverages you plan to try to continue to reduce "empty calories" from beverages?
- How did you get your family to drink more water?
- What was your family's reaction to the change in beverages?

Healthy Habit of the Month

Our nation's streets are lined with fast-food restaurants and convenience stores that house unhealthy food options. Our kids see countless advertisements on TV for processed foods and sugar-sweetened beverages. The average consumption of sweets and bakery desserts is about eight to 10 servings per week in 5- to 9-year-olds and 10- to 14-year-olds and six to eight servings per week in 15- to 19-year-olds. (American Heart Association)

A study published in *The Lancet* medical journal in 2004 found that those who frequently ate fast food gained 10 pounds more than those who did so less often and were more than twice as likely to develop an insulin disorder linked to diabetes. It has become so easy to access unhealthy food options that many Americans tend to make poor choices for their diets.

It might take a little more time to make a healthy turkey sandwich on whole-wheat bread than it does to drive through a fast-food restaurant. It might take a few extra minutes to wash and cut fresh vegetables than it does to grab a bag of potato chips. But the long-term impact of choosing healthy foods instead of junk foods is immeasurable.

For Your Discussion
- How often do you eat fast food or junk food like potato chips, candy, etc.? How often do your kids eat these things?
- What are some ways you can reduce the amount of junk food consumed in your home?
- Is there a day of the week when you can take time to prepare healthy foods in advance? If so, what would you prepare?
- What quick and healthy snacks do your kids enjoy? What are some snacks that you'd like to have them try?
- Share ideas to avoid junk foods that have worked in your home.

More of This Month's Easy Steps to Be Well
- Spend one night of the week packaging food to eat on the go.
- Keep a cooler in your car or a backpack/purse with snacks available while on the go.
- Prepare a healthy after-school snack each morning when you prepare your child's lunch. It will be a fast, healthy option to grab when they get home.
- Shop around the perimeter of the grocery store to help purchase healthier options.
- Fresh fruit is a fast food. Grab one on the go any time.
- Keep a bowl of fresh fruits on the kitchen table so they are easy to grab.
- Prepare your own meals. Cooking allows you to be in control of what goes into your meal and cut out added sodium, fat, and sugar.
- Does your family love chicken nuggets? Try making your own homemade baked chicken nuggets for a healthier version.
- Substitute fresh fruit and veggies with peanut butter for your afternoon bag of chips.

More of This Month's Resources
- **Publication**: *The Cleaner Plate Club*, Beth Bader, Ali Benjamin
- **Mobile app**: CookWell
- **Organization**: Real Time Farms, www.realtimefarms.com

Notes

6 Go Green:
Increase Fruits and Vegetables

RECAP OF LAST MONTH
- What Easy Steps to Be Well were you able to implement last month?
- How did your family react to a reduction in junk food?
- What new foods did you discover that your kids liked?
- What timesaving tips can you share that helped your family eat healthier, real foods?

Healthy Habit of the Month

Only about 20 percent of high school students report eating fruits or vegetables more than the recommended five times per day. This alarming statistic is reflective of the vast majority of the American population's need to increase the amount of fruits and veggies in their diets.

Get creative with ways to incorporate more of these healthy foods in your diet. Make fresh fruits and veggies ready and available to your kids for snacking. Add these healthy foods to your family's favorite recipes by tossing them into pasta sauces, lasagna, casseroles, soups, and omelets. Have your kids try foods at least three times so they can try vegetables different ways. Eat foods that are ripe and in season.

If you teach your kids to love fruits and vegetables, they'll be more likely to consume the recommended amount of those foods as adults. Just think: By serving tasty foods like apples, grapes, strawberries, carrots, or green beans with every meal, you could be preparing your kids for a lifetime of good habits.

For Your Discussion

- What are your family's favorite fruits and vegetables?
- How often do your kids consume fruits and veggies? How often do you?
- What creative ways can you think of to make eating fruits and vegetables fun?
- What are some fruits and vegetables your family has never tried?

More of This Month's Easy Steps to Be Well

- Start your own garden and grow your own food. Find tips at www.gardenguides.com.
- Replace some of your favorite comfort foods with healthy veggies, such as replacing mashed potatoes with mashed cauliflower.
- Serve fruits and veggies in a fun way: Put fruit on a skewer, make veggie art, or serve foods in muffin tins to make it fun.
- Fruits have a plethora of vitamins and minerals. Try to include a fruit in your family's breakfast every single morning.
- Not a fan of spinach? Throw some in a blender with a frozen banana, milk, and peanut butter for a tasty treat without a hint of taste of the green stuff.
- Try to fill half of your plate with vegetables at lunch and dinner to make sure you're getting your quota for the day.
- Make a fruit salad for your family with seasonal produce. It makes a great side dish for breakfast, lunch, or dinner.
- Replace birthday cakes with nontraditional options like watermelon cakes.

More of This Month's Resources

- **Publication**: *The Vegetables We Eat*, Gail Gibbons
- **Mobile app**: Veggie Cookbook+
- **Organization**: Just Say Yes to Fruits and Vegetables, www.jsyfruitveggies.org and www.mealsmatter.org
- **In my community**: Your local farmers market

Notes

7

Limit All
Screen Time

RECAP OF LAST MONTH
- What Easy Steps to Be Well were you able to implement last month?
- How did your family react to the increase in fruits and vegetables?
- What new fruits and veggies did you discover that your kids liked?
- What tips can you share that helped your family eat more fruits and veggies?

Healthy Habit of the Month
Studies show that over the past five years, children and teens have increased the amount of time they spend watching TV and playing video and computer games to 7.5 hours — almost the same amount of time most adults spend at work each day.

Your child's total daily screen time may be greater than you realize. Start monitoring it, then take some simple steps to reduce the amount of time your child spends watching TV and movies or playing video or computer games. Screen time should be limited to an hour a day for children.

It is critical that parents understand the effects of too much screen time and how to enforce realistic limits. It will take some creativity and lifestyle changes to instill healthier screen time habits, but you'll find that kids will move more and stay healthier if you make these changes.

For Your Discussion
- How much screen time do your children get each day (including television, computers, video games, cellphones, and other digital media)?
- What else can your kids do for fun at home instead of watching TV or playing video games?
- Share ideas for games to play with your kids or activities that will get them away from screens.

More of This Month's Easy
Steps to Be Well
- Make a chart and award your child a star for every day that they don't watch TV.
- Listen to music and dance instead of watching TV.
- Set a timer to help measure 60 minutes of screen time for your family each day and stick to it.

- Limit cellphone, computer, and TV time before bed to ensure that your family gets a restful night's sleep.
- If you are not watching a specific program, turn off the TV. Eliminate the TV as background noise.
- Turn off the TV during family meals.

More of This Month's Resources
- **Publication**: *101 Offline Activities You Can Do With Your Child*, Steve Bennett, Ruth Bennett
- **Mobile app**: ActiveChannel
- **Organization**: ProActiveKids, www.proactivekids.org
- **In my community**: Playground at your local school

Notes

MONTH 8 Get Moving

RECAP OF LAST MONTH
• What Easy Steps to Be Well were you able to implement last month?
• How did your family react to the decrease in screen time?
• What new activities did you discover that your kids liked?
• What tips can you share that helped your family decrease screen time?

Healthy Habit of the Month

By now you've read that kids need a recommended 60 minutes of physical activity each day. Using the knowledge from last month about decreasing screen time should have helped you get over one of the biggest hurdles to increasing physical activity.

Now it's time to explore new activities and ideas to get your kids moving more. Doing things as a family will help you ensure you're all getting the amount of physical activity you need. Play tag together. Walk or ride bikes. Physical activity doesn't have to be something you dread. Find an activity you love and do it every day!

For Your Discussion

• What are some activities that your family enjoys doing together?
• What games can you play with your kids that involve moving more than sitting?
• Share ideas to get your family moving before and after school.

More of This Month's Easy Steps to Be Well

• Count your steps and buy a pedometer.
• Play outside with your kids instead of just telling them to go play alone. Challenge your kids to a game of four-square or hide-and-seek instead of letting them play video games.
• Respond to your child's needs. When your kids naturally need time to blow off steam, take advantage of their natural instinct to play and get moving with them.

• If your kids don't enjoy a particular activity like running, try playing outside together. Playing can be just as active as any sport.
• When watching a TV program, get up and do jumping jacks or sit-ups during the commercial breaks.
• Reward yourself for exercising each day — but avoid rewarding yourself with food.
• Weekends are for relaxing, but make sure you and your family aren't couch potatoes. Take a day trip to a lake to go kayaking or paddleboarding.
• Find activities you and your family can enjoy together. Hiking, tennis, and playing Frisbee are all fun, active reasons to get off of the couch.

More of This Month's Resources

• **Publication**: *Get Moving with Grover*, Louis Womble
• **Mobile app**: MapMyRUN
• **Organization**: YMCA, www.ymca.net
• **In my community**: Walk around the block or at the mall

Notes

9 Get More Sleep

RECAP OF LAST MONTH
- What Easy Steps to Be Well were you able to implement last month?
- Was your family able to increase physical activity last month? How?
- What new activities did you discover that your kids liked?
- What tips can you share that helped your family get moving?

Healthy Habit of the Month

In our discussions with different families, we determined that increasing hours of sleep was perceived as one of the hardest things for a busy family to increase. But in reality, your children can get more sleep by making some simple lifestyle changes that can get them to sleep faster, better, and for the recommended nine hours per night.

A good night's sleep is critical for good health. Making the healthy changes you've made thus far will also help your children sleep, including moving more and decreasing screen time. Having a TV in a child's bedroom has been associated with increased screen time, disrupted sleep, and an increased risk of obesity. In addition, the light from TV and computer screens in the bedroom can disturb sleep. Interrupted or restless sleep can increase the risk for overweight and obesity and can have other health and safety effects in people of all ages.

For Your Discussion
- What is your family's bedtime routine, if you have one?
- What keeps you and your child from getting good sleep at night?
- What immediate changes can you make to your child's bedtime routine?
- Are there things that help you sleep that you could try with your child?

More of This Month's Easy Steps to Be Well
- Go to bed at the same time every night.
- Make sleep a priority by keeping a consistent bedtime schedule and wake-up schedule; try to stick to it even on the weekends.
- Trouble sleeping? Try a relaxing bedtime routine such as a bubble bath, cup of hot tea, or listening to soothing music.
- Keep your room at a comfortable temperature, dark, and quiet for the best possible sleep environment.
- Keep electronics out of the bedroom.

More of This Month's Resources
- **Publication**: *The Good Sleep Guide*, Timothy Sharp
- **Mobile app**: Sleepy Time Sleep Timer
- **Organization**: The Better Sleep Council, www.bettersleep.org
- **In my community**: Your own bedroom

Notes

10

Make Friends
and Buddy Up

RECAP OF LAST MONTH
- Were you able to increase the amount of nightly sleep you got last month?
- How did your family respond to the increased amount of sleep? Did you notice behavior changes because of the increase?
- Do you have a new bedtime routine? What is it?
- What tips can you share that helped your child increase the amount of sleep he or she gets each night?

Healthy Habit of the Month
Wellness buddies can help you get more active and stick to your routine. Kids tend to be more physically active if their friends are active, too.

A physical activity buddy can help you stay active by making the time more fun and encouraging you to stick to your routine. Research suggests people may be more successful losing weight through physical activity when they have buddies or support partners.

Look for people who also want to be more active and whose company you enjoy. Involve friends, neighbors, family members, or other people you like to be with. Work together to figure out which types of activities, locations, and times work for all of you. Share recipes and ideas that work for your family. You can then motivate each other and stay committed to your healthy living goals.

For Your Discussion
- Who can you invite to be your wellness buddy?
- Do you know a couple or groups of people who've partnered in the past to make healthy lifestyle changes? What questions should you ask those people to help you and your buddies?
- Create a list of your child's friends who might be interested in being a wellness buddy and outline a plan to share with their parents.

More of This Month's Easy Steps to Be Well
- Pick an accountability partner and check in once a day via phone or text.
- Challenge your friends in a contest to log the most steps each week to increase the amount of walking you all do.
- Communicate your health goals to your friends and family — even extended family — so they can be supportive of you. Make being healthy a family affair!
- Instead of meeting up with friends over decadent meals, try planning a run or tennis match. You'll get to spend time with your loved ones and keep active.
- Try a group class at the gym to meet new friends with healthy, active lifestyles.
- Organize a team for a local 5K walk or run.

More of This Month's Resources
- **Publication**: "Better with a Buddy: Influence of Best Friends on Children's Physical Activity," *Medicine & Science in Sports & Exercise*, R. Jago, K. Macdonald-Wallis, J.L. Thompson, A.S. Page, R. Brockman, K.R. Fox.
- **Mobile app**: Fitness Buddy
- **Organization**: Friends' Health Connection, www.friendshealthconnection.org
- **In my community**: Your neighborhood park

11

Go to School

RECAP OF LAST MONTH
- What Easy Steps to Be Well were you able to implement last month?
- Who did you partner with last month? What was his/her response when you first asked him/her to be part of your wellness journey?
- What new activities did you discover that you liked to do together?
- How will you continue to work together in the future? Did you set similar goals? Did you set a regular meeting time?

Healthy Habit of the Month
On a typical school day, our children spend more waking hours at school than they do in any other location. Therefore, it is important that their school is a healthy environment. Did you know that by federal law, schools must have a wellness policy with goals for nutrition education, physical activities, and other school-based activities that promote wellness? Research shows that steady parent involvement at school leads to improved student achievement. You can help support healthy initiatives for families by leveraging the school's programming, facilities, and social opportunities. Help out at your child's school. It is a great way to learn more about the school environment and support wellness programs. There are many ways to help make your child's school a healthier place.

After-school programs are also a great way to get your children more active. An estimated 6.6 million youth participate in after-school physical activity programs. An additional 22 million families say they'd be interested in after-school programs if they were available.

You might want to explore the resources available at Alliance for a Healthier Generation's Healthy Schools Program, www.healthiergeneration.org, and help your school work toward being a healthier environment.

For Your Discussion
- What healthy programs already exist at your child's school? Can you volunteer to help with those programs?
- What healthy programs would you like to see implemented at your child's school?
- Who could be a healthy living champion at your child's school?

- How will you go about getting more involved at your child's school?

More of This Month's Easy Steps to Be Well
- Talk to the P.E. teacher, nurse, or health teacher to start a wellness program with other like-minded parents to rally for healthier choices.
- Investigate your school's lunch policies and practices. Start a letter writing campaign to integrate healthier foods into the lunch room.
- Submit some fun games to your child's teacher to help introduce new ways to get moving.
- Bring healthy snacks for your kid's classes once a month to introduce new fruits and veggies.
- Walk to and from school every day instead of driving.
- Encourage your kids to be leaders and help model good behavior at school.
- Don't let your children sit around on school breaks and after school; keep their minds and bodies active!
- Encourage nutrition education at your child's school. Contact the principal about initiating assemblies discussing healthy nutrition, habits, and activity.

More of This Month's Resources
- **Publication**: *Quick, Cheap and Healthy School Lunches That Your Kids Will Love!*, Jill Green, Daniel Kaplan
- **Mobile app**: School Snax Lite
- **Organization**: The Center for Health and Health Care in Schools, www.healthinschools.org, and Safe Routes to School, www.saferoutesinfo.org
- **In my community**: Your child's school

Notes

Pass It On:
Spark a Community Effort

RECAP OF LAST MONTH
- How were you able to get more involved in your child's school last month?
- How did your child react to you being at school?
- What activities or programs did you discover that are already offered at your school?
- What new activities did you recommend to the school?

Healthy Habit of the Month

People who live in communities where it is easy to walk, run, bike, and play move more. Easier access to fruits and vegetables will also increase the amounts of those healthy foods that are eaten by community members.

Half of American kids don't have a park, community center, or sidewalk in their neighborhood. But changes in local policies, zoning laws, and community efforts can make neighborhoods healthier. Working together, community members can implement creative ways to be more active and provide more healthy opportunities for children.

Parks can be cleaned up with your help and made safer for children. Unused spaces can be turned into playgrounds. Walking groups can be started with a group of friends and grow through grass-roots efforts.

It only takes one person to start making a difference in your community: you!

For Your Discussion
- What healthy programs are supported by community groups in your town?
- What resources are your community lacking that could lead to families living healthier lives? Do you need a new park? Does the neighborhood need a neighborhood watch program to ensure kids' safety?
- Does your neighborhood have a community garden? How can you get involved?
- Identify ways that you can impact your community.

More of This Month's Easy Steps to Be Well
- School committees are made up of concerned parents just like you. If you want to be heard and get involved, it's a great place to start.
- Start a community garden and share the responsibilities with your friends and neighbors.
- Create a healthy recipe swap among your community members.
- Start a Be Well walking group that meets each morning after you take your kids to school or each evening after work.
- Create a book club and discuss the book while you are walking around the neighborhood.
- Find a farmers market in your area and try to shop local whenever possible.
- Encourage local retailers and restaurants in your area to offer healthy food. Offer to help teach other consumers about healthy food choices.

More of This Month's Resources
- **Publication**: *Community Nutrition*, Nweze Nnakwe
- **Mobile app**: Food Community
- **Organization**: Community Garden, www.communitygarden.org
- **In my community**: Your local city hall

Notes

Finally **Reflect** and Re-Plan

- What are some of the community programs that you discovered last month?
- What additional needs for your community did you discover?
- What action did you take to start helping your community be a healthier one?

Healthy Habit of the Month

Congratulations! You've made it through a year of being well. You've likely made some big changes in your home over the past 12 months, and you should be proud of any healthy habits you and your family have adopted.

Now is the time to reflect on the successes you've had and map out a plan for the coming year. It will get even easier over time to implement and stick to your healthy habits.

Keep up the great work!

For Your Discussion

- What information and knowledge did you gain from *A Year of Being Well: Messages from Families on Living Healthier Lives* that was most helpful to you and your family?
- What healthy habits will you try to instill in the coming year?
- What tools do you think you need to help you be even more successful at living healthy in the coming year?

More of This Month's Easy Steps to Be Well

- Keep a journal — online or in hard copy — to track your success.
- Identify your weaknesses and replicate your strengths.
- Look at the calendar for the coming year and identify times when you might struggle to stay healthy. Look for resources to help teach you ideas on how to keep moving during those times of the year.
- As you reflect, know that nobody is perfect. Making mistakes is a part of the journey. Identify your missteps and do better in the year to come.
- Start *A Year of Being Well* from the beginning, and take on some of the Easy Action Steps you may not have incorporated last year.

More of This Month's Resources

- **Publication**: *52 Small Changes*, Brett Blumenthal
- **Mobile app**: Pocket Mentor
- **Organization**: National Institutes of Health, www.nih.gov
- **In my community**: Start a new journal